CATCH A FISH,

THROW A BALL, FLY A KITE

CATCH A FISH, THROW

 THREE RIVERS PRESS • NEW YORK

A BALL, FLY A KITE

21 TIMELESS SKILLS
EVERY CHILD SHOULD KNOW
(and Any Parent Can Teach!)

JEFFREY LEE

WITH ILLUSTRATIONS BY PHILOMENA O'NEILL

Published by Three Rivers Press, New York, New York.
Member of the Crown Publishing Group, a division of Random House, Inc.
www.crownpublishing.com

THREE RIVERS PRESS and the Tugboat design are registered trademarks of Random House, Inc.

Printed in the United States of America

Design by Lauren Dong
Illustrations by Philomena O'Neill

Library of Congress Cataloging-in-Publication Data
   Lee, Jeffrey, 1960–
      Catch a fish, throw a ball, fly a kite : twenty-one timeless skills every child should know (and any parent can teach!) / Jeffrey Lee.—1st ed.
   1. Family recreation.   2. Parent and child.   3. Life skills.   I. Title.
   GV182.8 .L44 2004
   790.1'91—dc22   2003016333

ISBN 1-4000-4810-9
10 9 8 7 6 5 4 3 2 1

First Edition

For my mom and dad,
who did so much, so well,
with so little help.

Acknowledgments

My deepest gratitude to Barbara Moravec, Joel ben Izzy, Dorian Karchmar, and Becky Cabaza, without whom this book might never have been written.

Thanks also to these people, who were so generous with their help at every step along the way: Madeline Lee, Juliana Lee, Marcus Rempel, Sandi Everlove, Hannah Rempel, Jodie Wohl, Alison Odell, Rob Saper, Al Russell, Dave Richardson, Julie Jenkins, Leroy Jenkins, Hailey Jenkins, Jamie Jenkins, Lisa Kartiganer, and Ani Schroeter.

Contents

CATCH A FISH,

THROW A BALL, FLY A KITE

INTRODUCTION

> "You don't spoil your kids by giving them what they want—you spoil them by giving them everything except what they want. What they want is you."
>
> —Jim McHugh

My father used to get them from the library. They were dog-eared paperbacks, held together by Scotch tape, with titles like *Figure Drawing Made Easy* or *Lucas on Bass Fishing* or *Bob Cousy's Guide to Winning Basketball.* After dinner he'd sit in his big brown recliner and study them page by page. I used to look over his shoulder at the pictures. Once in a while he'd point one out and explain it to me.

"See? You have to keep your arms up so they can't pass it over you."

"Look. That's where the big ones are—in the weeds, next to the sunken log."

Then he'd push his glasses onto the bridge of his nose and pore over the image—like a scholar deciphering an ancient scroll.

He had a tough job to do, and he knew it. Neither his childhood in China nor his adolescence in his family's laundry had prepared him to raise four sons who wanted to be all-American boys. His own parents, with their old world ways, had little parenting advice to offer. Nor did anyone else. Back then, *parent* wasn't even a verb.

So he went to the library, and he did the best he could. His sons wanted to play baseball? He came home after a long day's work and played catch. They wanted to go fishing? He got up at five in the morning, bundled us into the station wagon, and drove to the lake.

But somehow, the books never told him the things he really needed to know. How do you catch a pop fly without getting bonked on the head? How do you get a barbed fishhook out of your hand? He did his best, and he made it up as he went along. In a way, I wrote this book for him—only thirty years too late. It's the book he always needed but never had.

The funny thing is, I needed it even more than he did. When I first started parenting, I was pretty cocky. After all, my parents had done it with four unruly boys, and no guidance to speak of. *We* turned out okay, didn't we? How hard could it be?

Famous last words.

The first time I tried to teach my daughter something, I made her cry. It was a long time before we actually started having fun. But once we did, it was *lots* of fun—more, in fact, than I ever could have imagined. And in the end that's what this book is about. You and your kids are going to have a great time with this stuff—maybe even better than I did, since you won't have to repeat all my mistakes.

The biggest mistakes always came from my ignorance about how kids really learned. Those are mistakes you can avoid. Let me pass on a few useful tips I figured out along the way.

SEE ONE, DO ONE, TEACH ONE

There's a little secret about doctors that most people would just as soon not know. In our early training, most of what we learned was passed down, not from sage, gray-haired Marcus Welby look-alikes, but from young doctors who were only one step ahead of us in their training. The tongue-in-cheek name we had for this arrangement was "See one, do one, teach one," though we took great pains not to utter it in front of the patient on whom the lesson was taking place.

Clearly, this isn't the ideal way to learn medicine. But having taken part in the system as both student and teacher, I've seen it work much better than you'd expect. The reason is simple:

You don't have to be an expert to be a good teacher.

Did you ever try to teach a beginner something that you've known how to do for a very long time? You think that all you need to do is demonstrate a couple of times and they'll see how simple it is. But somehow it doesn't work out that way. They ask you to explain the things you usually do without thinking. Pretty soon you realize that you don't know *how* you do this thing at all—you just do it. And the more you try to break it down and explain it, the more awkward and unnatural it seems.

To teach a beginner, you need to have *beginner's mind.* You have to know how strange and new it all feels—how every turn of the head and gesture of the hand is unfamiliar ground. Of course, experience has its advantages, but no one understands *beginner's mind* like someone who has recently been a beginner.

So relax. You don't need to be an expert. And the worst thing you can do is try to act like one when you're not. Learning comes quicker and easier when you aren't afraid to make mistakes. Model that for your kids. Show them how to take chances, fall flat on your face, and get up laughing. Sometimes the bloopers are the parts we enjoy the most.

KNOW YOUR KID

The other reason beginners can be good teachers is that they don't spend all their time pontificating and showing off. The most important thing about teaching is observing. The very fact that you are watching and listening will transform the way your children learn. Your caring helps them focus. Your focus makes them care.

But what, exactly, are you supposed to observe?

The most important thing you need to find out is who your kid is, and what he's ready to do. It sounds so simple—until you try it.

None of us are objective about our kids. We have hopes and dreams and lots of expectations that cloud our ability to see who they really are. But if you want to take them on a journey, you have to start out wherever they are at that moment. Try to see them clearly—not to judge, but just to know.

Are they graceful and swift, or a little clumsy? Do they learn easily, or do they have to work at it? Do they stick to a task like glue, or do they wander and lose interest? How is their strength? Their endurance? Their memory? Their self-confidence?

Teach the kid in front of you, not the kid you wish she would be. It saves everyone a lot of frustration. And when you know exactly where she started, you can tell when she makes progress, no matter how small it is. Progress is always worth celebrating. Why miss out on anything so sweet?

Once you think you know who your kid is, you still have to watch him closely. Children are notorious shape-shifters. Emotions wash through them like waves, and there always seems to be a new one on the way. Are they nervous? Excited? Tired? Scared? Learn to read your kids from moment to moment, and you'll have a much better idea what they need. Sometimes it's encouragement, or reassurance. Sometimes it's a rest, or a tickle fight. And sometimes it's time to call it a day. If you stop while it's still fun, you're sure to be out there again soon.

GIVE THEM WHAT THEY WANT

In education circles there's a lot of talk about learning styles. For the most part, that's a good thing. Every kid is different, and the better we are at recognizing those differences, the better we'll be at teaching our kids. But the last thing you want to do is pigeonhole your children, and thus limit your options as a teacher. I come from a tradition of Chinese pragmatism, and as far as I'm concerned, you should do whatever works.

What works when you're teaching kids can change from kid to kid, from skill to skill, and from moment to moment. That's because children, like all of us, have many reasons for the things they do—sometimes several all at once. If you can figure out what's motivating them at a given moment, you can put the biggest, tastiest carrot at the end of the stick. After that, everything goes smoother.

So what is it that motivates kids? Not surprisingly, the same things that motivate you and me. But remember, they may not have those motivations in the same amounts at the same time. Here are a few things that make kids want to learn:

Mastery

Almost everyone gets satisfaction from doing things well, and kids are no exception. The problem is, grown-ups often focus on achievement as the only goal, whereas kids think of it as one of many. Moreover, adults sometimes pay attention only to the final results, while kids can take pride in smaller achievements along the way.

In every chapter of this book you'll find step-by-step instructions for learning a new skill. Remember, each step is an accomplishment all by itself—and therefore a chance to tell your kid how well he is doing, and how proud you are. There are dozens of chances like that in learning any skill. Don't let them pass you by.

Fun

If grown-ups tend to be goal-oriented, kids are just as strongly fun-oriented. For them, this is the ultimate litmus test. If they're not having fun, your choices for keeping them engaged boil down to intimidation and physical restraints. Luckily, all of the activities in this book have an inherently high fun quotient. But that doesn't mean you can ignore it. Learning something new is hard work, and it's often frustrating. It's up to you to make sure the scales are tipped toward fun.

The first rule of keeping it fun is the most obvious, and the most often neglected. *You have to have fun yourself.* If your attitude is grim and single-minded, don't expect your kids to have a barrel of laughs. Lighten up a little. Most of these chapters include jokes, riddles, and games. When the mood starts to drag, give them a try. Or just make silly faces and run around with a lamp shade on your head. Be creative. This book is an invitation for you to act like a kid again. That's an offer you can't refuse.

Curiosity

We humans are a lot more like monkeys than we like to admit. We have short attention spans, and a propensity for mischief if we're left alone too long. But if you can arouse our curiosity, you'll have us eating bananas right out of your hand. Kids, especially, are endlessly curious about the world around them. They're always asking questions, especially: "Why?" Just once, wouldn't you like to have an intelligent response?

Throughout this book, I've sprinkled lots of fun facts, odd trivia, and scientific explanations. Even if they don't answer the questions your kids have, they answer a few they never thought of, and that's almost as good. Besides, they'll make you look a little smarter than you really are. What parent doesn't need *that* once in a while?

Love

This is it—your ace in the hole! No matter how much your kids are driven by those other motivations, this is the one that will keep them coming back for more. They want *you*. And by reading this book, and picking out some things to do with them, you've given them something that no sports camp, after-school program, or private tutor ever can. So while you're watching that follow-through, or kneading that bread dough, or feeling that first fish tug on the line, don't forget the reason you're doing all this in the first place.

Enjoy their company. Notice how small their hands are. Ask them what they think about before they fall asleep. Tell them what it was like when you were a kid. And most of all, tell them you love them. Say it out loud, every way you know how to say it, again and again and again. They never get tired of it. They never hear it too much.

Okay, who's pontificating now? Enough of my blather—it's time to get on with the good stuff. Grab your kids, plop down on the sofa, and start flipping pages. See how happy they are just doing that? You haven't even started, and the good stuff has already begun.

1
CATCH A FISH

*"Give a man a fish, and he eats for a day. Teach a man to
fish, and you're lucky if he even comes home for dinner."*
                                                    —Anonymous

When I was growing up, the only time I had my father all to myself was when we were fishing. My brothers fished too, but they weren't obsessed with it, like my dad and I. He'd creep into my room before dawn to tap me on the shoulder, and I'd wake up instantly, as if I'd been waiting for that moment all night long. Then we'd sneak out of the house together and load up the car in the dark.

We'd reach the lake with the sky aglow in the east and the birds just beginning to sing. Often, we'd hear the faint sound of a splash across the cove.

"You hear that?" my dad would whisper. "They're hungry!"

After that he wouldn't say much. That's how he was—more comfortable with silence than conversation. That was fine with me. I was happy just to sit with him by the water and watch the sun come up over the trees.

Years later, when I was in medical school, I came home one weekend for a visit. Since my brothers and I had moved out, my father had gone on to new interests, and our little rowboat hadn't gotten much use. On a whim I asked him to go fishing with me.

He came to wake me an hour before dawn, and I was up as soon as he tapped my shoulder. That morning the fish really *were* hungry. In just a couple of hours we caught a stringer-full of fat bass. We headed home early, triumphant hunters, with the quiet of early morning still hanging in the air.

I was surprised when my father broke the silence.

"You know," he said, "we probably didn't tell you this enough, but your mom and I have always been very proud of you and the things you've done."

I turned to look at him, but he was staring straight ahead. Behind him the sun flashed and flickered on the lake as we drove along the shore.

"That's okay," I said. "I knew."

WHEN TO START

There's no easy answer to this one. Mostly, it depends on your kids. If they love being outdoors and they're fascinated by little critters, fishing is an easy sell. But remember, the younger they are, the shorter their attention spans. Fishing can involve a lot of waiting, and some kids aren't good at that. Later on I'll give you some tricks to keep their interest, but you still have to be realistic about how long they can sit in one place. If you think they can hang in there for at least an hour, then give it a try.

WHAT YOU NEED BEFORE YOU START

A Place to Fish

This is the most important part of your preparation. When you take a kid fishing for the first time, you're looking for one thing, and one thing only: *action!* What you want is a place where there are lots of hungry little fish to gobble up anything you dangle in front of them. The key is to go after the fish that serious fishermen ignore. These are called panfish.

Panfish are the little fish that gather in the shallows of lakes and ponds. They're the perfect quarry for beginners. The most common are little members of the bass family, known collectively as sunfish. They all have the same rounded shape and seldom grow much larger than eight inches. Also common is the yellow perch. There may be others in your particular region, but sunfish and perch can be found almost anywhere. They're good eating and easy to catch.

Some ponds and lakes are stocked heavily with hatchery fish, usually trout. This is a good choice too, especially at the beginning of the fishing season, but you may have to fight the crowds.

To locate a good fishing spot, call up a local bait shop or fishing tackle store. You can also try your state Fish and Game Department. Tell them you want to take your kid where it's easy to catch small fish. Ask if there's a dock or a clear stretch of shoreline where a beginner can cast without getting hung up in the trees. You probably want to stay away from boats with younger kids, both for safety's sake and to allow a quick getaway if they get cranky and want to go home.

I've suggested ponds and lakes because rivers and saltwater are often harder to fish, but there may be exceptions where you live. In any case, check out whatever spot you choose before you actually go fishing, to make sure it's both safe and accessible.

One last alternative is to find a local "U-Fish" place. These are private ponds where you pay to catch stocked fish. They can be expensive and crowded, and they won't give you much of an outdoor experience. On the other hand, you'll usually catch something—and your first time out with a kid, that's a big advantage.

Fishing License

Every state has its own regulations on who needs a license, where and when they can fish, and what they can fish for. You can buy a license at most tackle or bait shops, but call ahead to make sure. A booklet with your state's regulations should come with the license.

Equipment

There's no end to the amount of equipment you can buy in the name of catching fish. For diehards like me, that's half the fun. But to start with, you need only a few basics.

• *Rods and reels*. These come in a dizzying range of shapes, sizes, and prices. As you get into bigger fish and special conditions, you'll need better equipment. But for little fish and quiet water, it almost doesn't matter. For your first attempt at fishing, this is what you should do.

Walk into any discount department store that carries fishing equipment. Buy a couple of cheap, lightweight rods and spinning reels with the fishing line already on them. The rod and reel are often sold together as a combo. Get one of the shorter, thinner rods—it should be flexible and whippy, so even little fish will give it a good bend. Don't get the *really* cheap one that looks like a toy. Get the next cheapest one that looks like a real fishing rod.

If your kid is younger than six, you might get a combo with a spin-cast reel. The push-button mechanism is a little easier to handle, and the covering over the spool is supposed the keep the line from getting tangled. On the other hand, regular spinning reels cast much farther and aren't that much harder to use. And with a child that young, you'll probably end up casting for her anyway.

• *Hooks*. Get a box of number 10 hooks. The larger the number, the

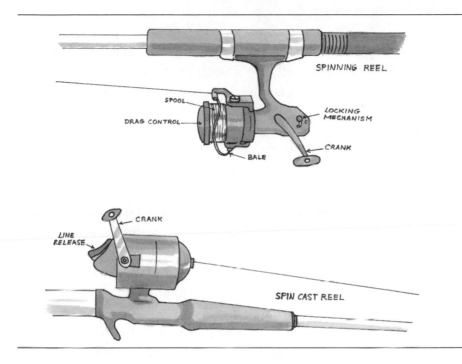

smaller the hook, and these are pretty small. Remember, little fish have little mouths.

• *Sinkers.* Buy a box of small, round, split-shot sinkers. Get the ones that are about the size of small green peas, with the little wings on the back that make them easier to open and close.

• *Bobbers.* Get at least four red-and-white plastic floats, also known as bobbers. The bigger the bobber, the harder it is for a fish to pull it under, so get small ones. About an inch in diameter should do.

• *Extra line.* Get a spool of cheap replacement line. Four-pound test strength would be more than enough for little fish, but six-pound will help you pull free from weeds and snags.

• *Tackle box.* Actually, a shoe box would be sufficient, but a small plastic tackle box doesn't cost much. It helps keep your stuff organized, it has a handle for easy carrying, and it makes you feel like a fisherman.

• *Other stuff.* All of the following will come in handy: nail clippers, needle-nosed pliers, a pocketknife, a bucket with a handle, a few rags. If you live in an area with lots of mosquitoes or black flies, bring some bug juice that's safe for kids. And don't forget a camera to record the first catch for posterity.

Bait

There are lots of artificial lures that will catch fish, but they all require repeated casting. When kids first start fishing, casting is the source of most problems. Lines get tangled, people get impaled, trees get snagged—you get the idea. For a first fishing experience, especially when you're after little fish, bait is the way to go.

I've caught fish on everything from cheese balls to strips of bacon fat, but your best bet is probably that old standby, the common earthworm. For whatever reason, even fish that have never seen a worm instinctively know that it's good to eat. You can buy worms at a bait shop, but I recommend collecting your own. Kids have as much fun catching worms as they do catching fish.

You can dig up a supply of worms in any rich soil—a garden or compost pile are both good bets. These days, many people keep worm bins to process their kitchen waste. (See *Chapter 18: Grow a Garden* if you want to try it yourself.) The little red worms in these bins make great bait.

During the summer you can go out at night with flashlights and gather the big worms called nightcrawlers. They come out onto your lawn to mate. Your kids will love hunting for them, but whole nightcrawlers are too big for small panfish, so you may have to cut them up.

There's a novel way to catch worms that's sure to be a hit with your kids. If you drive a stake into reasonably wormy ground and then whack it with a stick, any worms that are right beneath the surface will come to the top. I've never heard an explanation for this, but my guess is that the vibrations make them think it's raining, so they come up to avoid the flood. In any case, give it a try. You won't get enough to fill your bait container, but your kids will be very impressed.

It's best to collect your worms the day before you fish. Put them in a plastic container with a little moist earth and some moss or grass on top. Punch a few breathing holes in the lid, and store them in the refrigerator, clearly marked so no one mistakes them for cottage cheese.

For the squeamish, bait is also sold in jars at bait and tackle shops. I don't recommend the preserved salmon eggs, because they don't stay on the hook, but the brightly colored "dough" baits like *Power Bait* can be very effective. They're especially good for hatchery raised trout that are used to eating food pellets.

Diversions

With a little planning you can have a great time even if the fish aren't biting. When was the last time you just sat beside your kid in a beautiful place and enjoyed her company? If that isn't "quality time," what is?

Bring along a book to read out loud. Or maybe a field guide to local trees and wildlife. Lean the rods over a branch and take a short walk. When you get far enough away to not scare the fish, turn to Chapter 12 and practice skipping stones. Look for animal shapes in the clouds, or animal tracks on the ground. Tell some stupid jokes from the end of this chapter. Enjoy the luxury of being together with time on your hands.

Whatever you do, don't forget to bring food and drink. Nothing tastes as good as food eaten outdoors. And bring along a little candy or some other treat for a surprise. Make it an occasion.

BASIC TECHNIQUE

Step 1: Rigging your line

The day before you go fishing, take out your rods and reels and get them set up. Kids love having their own rod, and rigging it up early not only helps out later, it starts the excitement a day ahead of time. Have them sit beside you and copy what you do.

• *Put the rod together.* Usually, a rod comes in two sections. Put them together and line up the guide loops so they're all on the same side. From this point on, remind your kid to be very careful about the tip of the rod—it breaks easily, and it has a nasty way of wagging around right at eye level.

• *Thread the line.* Take a look at the spinning reel (see drawing). The metal bar is called a bale. It keeps the line from unraveling freely, and guides it back onto the spool when you reel. Pull a couple feet of line off the spool and bring it under the bale.

On the body of the reel is a little lever that has two positions. With the lever in the locked position, the reel will turn in only the direction that reels in line. When it's in the unlocked position, you can turn the handle either way. Unlock the lever to let out some line.

Thread the line through the guide loops along the rod. The reel will be turning slowly as it lets out line. When you get past the last guide loop, pull off another few feet of line, then click the lever to stop the reel from letting out any more.

If you have some time and enough open space, it's a great idea to practice casting. Just attach a few sinkers to the end of the line and skip ahead to the section on casting. Try aiming your casts at different targets and a variety of distances. Just the act of casting can be a lot of fun, and the skill you gain will be a big help once you get on the water. But if time is in short supply, continue rigging your line.

• *Tie on a hook*. Thread the line through the eyelet of a hook and twist the hook around several times. Bring the loose end of the line through the loop beside the hook, and tighten the knot by pulling the line from both sides (see drawing). This is called a "clinch knot." Trim the loose end to about a quarter inch, using your teeth or a nail clipper. Obviously, the hooks are sharp, so this is a task for grown-ups or older kids.

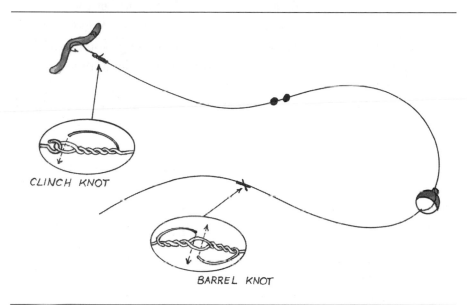

CLINCH KNOT

BARREL KNOT

• *Attach sinkers*. About a foot above the hook, use some needle-nosed pliers to pinch on a couple of sinkers. These will get the bait down to where the fish are.

• *Attach a bobber*. If the fish are on the bottom, you may end up using sinkers alone. However, there are a lot of weeds and snags down there to get hung up on, and bobbers help you avoid them. Also, a bobber gives your kid something tangible to watch and allows her to see every little nibble with her own eyes. That alone makes it worth using.

Press down the button at the top of the bobber until the little wire hook comes out the other end, and loop it around the line above the sinkers. Now, while using your finger to keep that hook in place, press the edge of the button down so the little hook at the other end of the wire pops up in the button's middle (see drawing). Run the line under that hook and release the button. Now the line is attached at both ends of the bobber.

You should still be able to slide the bobber to adjust the depth of your bait, but it should be attached firmly enough so it doesn't move around when you cast. When you're actually fishing, you'll place the bobber about two or three feet above the sinkers, depending on how deep you want to fish.

• *Set your drag*. Drag is the adjustment on the reel that allows a big fish to pull line off the reel when it makes a strong run, instead of breaking the line. Since you won't be fishing for anything big enough to break your line, it's probably easiest to set the drag tight. The adjustment is at the front of the reel over the spool of line, or at the very back. On a spin-cast reel, it's usually a star-shaped wheel at the base of the crank (see drawing). Turn the drag adjustment until it's hard to pull line off the reel.

Step 2: Getting ready to go

Put the hook around the guide loop closest to the reel, with the point turned in. Slowly reel in enough line to take up the slack; enough to barely bend the tip of the rod. If the lever is in the locked position, as it should be, the line will stay tight. Lean the rod somewhere safe where it won't get stepped on. Tomorrow you go fishing!

Fish usually bite better when it's cool, especially in the heat of summer. That's one reason to go early in the morning. The other, more important reason is that early morning is a magical time to be up and around. It'll feel like something special to your kids—because it is.

In order to get an early start, have all your stuff ready to go. You might want to pack the car the night before, or make a checklist of everything you need to bring. There's nothing worse than driving all the way to the lake only to discover that your lunch and your bait are still in the refrigerator back home.

Step 3: Baiting the hook

Once you've found your spot, with plenty of room for casting, the first order of business is baiting your hook. You may want to do this for your kids, unless they feel comfortable handling a sharp hook and a slimy, wiggly worm.

Your worms will be sitting at the bottom of your plastic container. Gently coax one out and hold it between your thumb and forefinger. With your other hand, take the hook on the end of your line and pierce the middle of the worm. Rather than going all the way through, thread the point down the center of the worm and come out on the same side until the barb is showing.

Some worms have a pale thickening, or collar, about a third of the way down their body. Don't hook this spot, or the worm will die quickly and will be much less enticing to the fish.

You'll have to repeat this procedure whenever a worm is cast off, nibbled off, or looks waterlogged and limp.

If you use one of those dough baits from a jar, just pinch off a pea-sized piece and mold it around the hook, leaving the point exposed. It's cleaner and simpler than a worm, but it may not be as effective.

Step 4: Casting

The goals of casting are simple: a little distance, reasonable accuracy, bait that stays on the hook, and no one getting impaled. As I mentioned before, it's a good idea to practice ahead of time with sinkers before you do it with hooks.

You may have seen experienced fishermen cast artificial lures by whipping their rods back and forth directly overhead. This is not what we'll be doing. A cast like that is hard to control, and it's likely to send your carefully rigged worm flying off the hook in several pieces.

To begin, stand sideways to the water with your left foot forward. Since inexpensive reels all have the crank on the same side, you'll do it this way even if you're a lefty. Hold the rod in your right hand with the stem of the reel between your middle and ring fingers. Turn the handle until the bobber is about a foot from the rod tip, and stop when the bale brings the line near the handle of the rod.

Reach out with your right index finger and curl it around the line to hold it in place. Now take your left hand and pull back the bale so it clicks into the open position.

Keeping your eye on your worm so it doesn't drag along the ground, swing your rod tip back until it points away from the water.

You can grab the bottom of the rod handle with your left hand if it gives you better control. Now, with a sweeping motion like a tennis forehand, swing the rod tip forward and upward (see drawing).

Just as your rod tip points forward, straighten your index finger and release the line. Finish with your rod tip pointing directly above where you want your cast to land. Your whole rig should sail off in a gentle arc and land in the water with a soft plop.

Crank the handle forward (counterclockwise) until the bale flips back into the closed position. Now you're ready to fish.

As you teach your kids to cast, you can start out by putting your arms around them from behind, with your hands on top of theirs. Emphasize these points:

1. Always watch the back-cast so it doesn't hook anyone.
2. Let go of the line just as the rod points forward.
3. Point the rod where you want the cast to land.

If you're using a spin-cast reel, the motion is the same. Just push down the button during the back-cast, then let go of it to release the line as the rod points forward.

Step 5: Hooking a fish

If you're going to catch some fish, the first thing you have to do is find them. Hopefully, you've done your homework and found a lake or pond full of hungry panfish. But even if there are lots of fish, they won't be dispersed evenly all over a pond.

Most of the time, fish only care about two things: finding food and not becoming food. This means they hang around where there's something to eat and where they can duck under cover at a moment's notice. Cover could be almost anything: a big rock, a sunken tree, some floating lily pads, or even the dock you're sitting on. What it doesn't mean is open water with a flat sandy bottom.

Unfortunately, good cover can also mean snagged hooks and tangled lines. This is where a good, accurate cast can do wonders. Initially, cast to a spot where the bobber will suspend the bait above some underwater cover. Once your confidence improves, you can try casting closer to potential snags. If you don't like your first cast, reel it in and try again.

Once the lines are in the water, you can sit back and watch those bobbers. This is a good time to get out some food, or some other diversion. If you go fifteen or twenty minutes without a nibble, try reeling in the line, a little at a time, to attract attention. Check to see that the bait is still lively and free of weeds, and cast to a new spot.

When a fish bites, it will be obvious. The bobber will start moving erratically and bobbing up and down as if it's alive. If the bobber stays underwater or starts to move continuously, the fish has the bait firmly in its mouth. Reel in the slack line and lift the rod tip up in the air. With little fish, it's better not to set the hook with a big jerk of the rod—you'll probably just pull the hook out of the fish's mouth.

If the bobber dips down a couple of times then goes still, the fish is nibbling. Try twitching your line or reeling in slowly to make your worm look like it's trying to escape. This may trigger a more aggressive strike. If you reel your line all the way in and the bait is gone, put on a smaller piece of worm and hook it more firmly, then cast to the same spot and try again.

Sometimes the fish are cruising around on the bottom and your bait isn't getting down to them. You can lower the bait by sliding the bobber up the line, but if you go too far it's difficult to cast. The other option is to add a couple more sinkers to the line and take off the bobber.

When you cast out a sinking rig, let it go all the way to the bottom.

Reel in the slack very slowly to avoid dragging the hook through the rocks and weeds. When almost all the slack is gone, lean the rod securely over a branch or some other support. Since there's no bobber to watch, you'll look for a pull on the line or a twitch at the tip of the rod.

Step 6: Bringing it in

Landing little fish is easy. Point the rod upward at a 45-degree angle. Reel steadily until the bobber is near the tip of the rod. Then lift the fish gently onto the boat, dock, or shore. Don't use a net, like they do for bigger fish—it isn't necessary, and it's sure to get tangled up.

Step 7: Now what?

Once you catch a fish, use your needle-nosed pliers to gently extract the hook. Now you have a few options. You may want to talk this over with your kid ahead of time, since it can be a difficult decision.

• After you take a quick photo for a keepsake, handle the fish as little as possible and slip it back into the water. This is called catch and release. It causes the least amount of trauma to the fish, and it lets you avoid cleaning your catch. On the other hand, some feel that this reduces fishing to a pointless, gratuitous act. That's especially true if the fish swallows the bait and you have to pull the hook out of its throat or stomach, after which it is unlikely to survive.

• You can put the fish in a bucket of water and let your kid watch it swim around for a while before you let it go. This is a little more traumatic for the fish, but a lot more fun for your kid. You can also do this if you intend to keep the fish, but your kid may start to think of it as a pet, which brings problems of its own.

• You can kill the fish immediately. If you plan to keep the fish, this is the most humane option, but it can be traumatic for your kid. When my daughter and I go fishing, we copy the Native American ritual of thanking the fish for giving up its life so that we may eat. It's a nice way to remember that food doesn't come from grocery stores but from other living things, and it reminds us of our place in the circle of life. The fastest way to kill a fish is to cut the little piece of flesh between the gills that connects the front of the belly with the bottom jaw, and then bend the head back to break the neck. A cooler full of ice will keep the fish fresh for the ride home.

TROUBLESHOOTING

Tangled Line

Generations of parents have spent untold hours of frustration untangling fishing lines. My father did it. I did it. You will be called upon to do it too. This is my advice: *just say no.* Life's too short, and your time and patience are too precious.

If it's a minor tangle, see if you can tease it apart by gently pulling a few loops out of the knot. If that doesn't work, just cut the line. Line is cheap, so bring extra. Wind up the cut line into a ball and put it somewhere it won't get in your way or strangle the wildlife. Rerig your line.

If there isn't enough line left on your reel, tie on the new line with a barrel knot (see diagram). Stick a twig through the spool of extra line as an axle. Have your kid hold the two ends of the twig and reel on as much as you need.

Snags

Everyone gets snagged sooner or later. It just means you're fishing where there's cover. No snags, no fish.

Hold the rod up over your head with the tip toward the sky and try to dislodge the hook with short, sharp jerks. Try walking up and down the shore to change the angle. If the hook is stuck fast, you have no choice but to break the line.

Point the rod tip toward the snag and reel in the slack. Either tighten the drag or hold the spool so it can't turn. Now, walk backward until the line breaks. If the snag is a weed or a soft twig, the hook may finally pull free, but look out for flying tackle if it does. After a snag, check for weak spots and frayed line near the hook. Cut off any damaged line and rerig.

Impalement

Obviously, prevention is the best option here. Make it an ironclad rule to look back and make sure everything's clear during every back-cast. It's also a good idea to rig and bait hooks when no one is holding the rod.

When I'm fishing with my kids, I like to use my pliers to press down the barb of the hook. You lose a few fish that way, but it makes it easier to unhook anything, including snags, deeply hooked fish, and little hands.

After the hook is out, some washing and a Band-Aid are usually all you need. However, it wouldn't be a bad idea to make sure everyone is up to date on their tetanus shot.

WHAT'S NEXT

Once you get the fishing bug, there's no end to how far you can take it. You and your kid can explore deeper or more remote water with boats, or learn new techniques for fishing in the ocean or in rivers. You can try new kinds of lures and go after bigger fish. But whatever you do, your experience in hooking and landing smaller fish will be a good start.

There are books on how to catch every kind of fish in every kind of water. Find out what's swimming around in the ponds and rivers near you, and take a trip to the bookstore or library. Sometimes dreaming about your next catch is as fun as the fishing itself.

SAFETY TIPS

By far the biggest hazard on any fishing trip is the water. Drownings are remarkably common in this country, and usually the result of simple carelessness. Never leave your child unattended near water, especially if it's deep. On a boat, everyone should wear a life vest at all times, and a nonswimmer should probably wear one on a dock or a pier. If you and your kid are around water on a regular basis, swimming lessons are a must.

Besides water, there are other hazards to consider. We've already mentioned the deadly back-cast, but it's worth repeating. On every cast, look back to see where your hook is going.

Occasionally, the fish themselves can cause injury. Some have teeth, and almost all have sharp spines in their fins and gills. When you're holding a fish, use a damp rag and don't let it flop around.

Another problem is sunburn, and with it the increased risk of skin cancer. For light-skinned people, sun block of at least SPF 15 is a must, and hats and long sleeves are a good idea.

One final danger is lightning. Every year a large percentage of lightning victims are foolish people who stay out in thunderstorms, far from cover, holding graphite and metal poles in their hands. In other words: fishermen and golfers. If the forecast calls for thunderstorms, postpone the trip, and at the first sign of thunder or lightning, go home.

CLEANING YOUR CATCH

This is a messy job, but for fishermen it's a welcome ritual at the end of a successful day. To do the job with minimal mess, all you need is a knife and a paper grocery bag.

The first step is to remove the scales. Open the paper bag and place it on a counter or the bottom of the sink. Grasp the fish by its head and hold it down partway inside the bag. Using a sharp knife held perpendicular to the fish, remove the scales by scraping from the tail end toward the head. Turn the fish over so you can scale both sides, as well as the belly and back. If the fins are getting in the way, you can remove them with a pair of kitchen shears.

Once the scales are removed, use a sharp knife or some kitchen shears to open the fish's belly. Remove all organs, and scrape off the dark red kidney stripe that adheres to the spine. Rinse inside and out. Remove all gills, and remove the head if you wish.

You'll notice that once you've done all this, there isn't much left. It takes a lot of panfish to feed a family. But even if all you get is hors d'oeuvres, they'll be ones that your kid remembers for a long time.

"FRY THEM SUCKERS UP"

Some kids develop a taste for fish, and some don't. Here's a simple way of preparing panfish that gives you a decent chance with most kids.

After scaling and cleaning your catch, pat each fish dry, inside and out, with a paper towel. Find a plastic bag with no holes in it and put in half a cup of flour, a quarter teaspoon of salt, and a pinch or two of black pepper. You can add a little garlic powder too, if you like. Put your fish in the bag, seal it up, and shake until all the fish are well coated.

Fill a heavy skillet with vegetable oil to a depth of about a half an inch. Turn the heat to medium high and wait until it just begins to smoke. Slide in a few of your panfish so they lie in the pan without touching, being very careful not to splatter yourself with hot oil. Cook until golden brown on both sides, turning as needed.

Serve plain, or with a little fresh lemon. Remind everyone to look out for sharp little bones.

FUN FISHY FACTS

• The longest salmon migration takes place in the Yukon River, where some fish travel more than two thousand miles upstream from the Bering Sea.

• The biggest fish is the whale shark. It can reach a length of more than fifty feet and weigh several tons.

• The smallest fish is the goby. A fully-grown adult is less than half an inch long.

• The fastest fish is the sailfish, which has been clocked at speeds of up to seventy miles per hour.

FISHY ANATOMY

If you're squeamish, cleaning your catch is never going to be your favorite task. But if you're not faint of heart, it doesn't have to be a chore. Let your kid watch and think of it as a chance to show her some cool stuff. Fish have amazing adaptations that allow them to live underwater. This is a great opportunity to see them up close.

Look at the shape of the fish's body. It's sleek and aerodynamic—built for low resistance and speed. The dorsal fin adds stability, like a keel, and the tail provides thrust and steering. The other fins allow fine adjustments while swimming slowly or hovering in place.

The eyes are on either side of the head, and they protrude a little.

This gives the fish nearly 360 degrees of vision, allowing it to see predators and prey in any direction.

The fish's skin is covered with hard scales for protection and an outer layer of slime to fight off bacteria and fungus. When you catch and release a fish, you should try not to handle it too much. If you remove too much slime, the fish will be vulnerable to infection.

Along the side of the fish there is a horizontal line that runs from head to tail. This marks a special organ that allows the fish to sense vibrations in the water. It's just as important to a fish as our ears are to you and me.

Lift up the hard gill plate to see the feathery, pink gills underneath. They have lots of folds that increase their surface area. This allows the gases in the water to flow in and out of the fish's bloodstream. Oxygen comes in and carbon dioxide goes out, just as it does in our own lungs. The gills are red because of the rich blood supply needed to carry those gases.

When you open up the fish's belly, take a look at each organ. If the fish was killed recently, the heart may still be beating. The stomach may hold undigested food, still recognizable as insects or tiny fish. If it's breeding season, you may even find eggs or sacs of sperm.

See if you can find a smooth, white, cigar-shaped organ that looks and feels like a little balloon. This is called the air bladder. The fish fills it with gas to achieve neutral buoyancy. That means it can rest at any depth without sinking or floating. Submarines have air tanks that do the same thing—but fish figured it out a few million years before we did.

FISHY JOKES AND RIDDLES

Q: What did the fish say when she swam into a wall?
A: "Dam!"

Q: Why do some fish live only in saltwater?
A: Because pepper water makes them sneeze.

Q: What do you get if you cross an elephant with a fish?
A: Swimming trunks!

Q: How do you stop fish from smelling?
A: Plug up their noses.

Q: What do fish look like without eyes?
A: Fsh!

Q: There were two fish in a tank. What did one say to the other?
A: "Let me drive, and don't fire the cannon unless I say so."

Q: What kind of fish tastes good with a peanut butter sandwich?
A: A jellyfish!

Q: How do you catch a computer fish?
A: First you get it online, then you use the Net.

Q: What kind of fish can jump higher than a building?
A: Any kind. Buildings can't jump.

2
THROW A BALL

"I know a lot of women who can throw harder and better than a normal male. It's not gender that makes a difference, it's how they throw."

—Linda Wells, Coach,
Arizona State University softball team

For me, it was a matter of pride. No daughter of mine was going to grow up "throwing like a girl."

I know—I'm not supposed to say that. It's not at all politically correct. But it's a term that never seems to die, because everyone knows exactly what it means. We've all seen it—that pathetic little hop and push that ends with the ball dribbling to a stop a few feet from where it was thrown. Of course boys do it too, but it's much more common in girls, because no one bothers to teach them how to throw. And as long as that's true, people are always going to call it "throwing like a girl."

This year, my daughter Madeline played her first season of Little League. We worked on her throw for a few minutes almost every day. By the end of the year she was making the long toss from third base to first like she'd been doing it all her life. And best of all, she was loving it.

At the end of the season her whole team got tickets for Little League Day at a Seattle Mariner's game. We were standing around watching the pitchers warm up when a man with a walkie-talkie tapped me on the shoulder.

"Hey, is that your daughter?"

"Yeah. Why?"

"I'm with the Mariners promotions department. Every year, on Little League Day, we have one of the kids throw out the first pitch. You think your daughter might be interested?"

Half an hour later I watched my little girl walk alone onto the field in front of 45,000 screaming fans and throw a perfect strike to the Mariner Moose. As she jogged back off, her smile was about thirty feet wide on the giant scoreboard screen. I ask you, if that's not parenthood nirvana, what is?

WHEN TO START

Kids start throwing objects on their own at all different ages. My youngest daughter is three, and she can already hit me with a Lego from across the room. There's nothing wrong with encouraging throwing as soon as it starts, but most kids won't have the body awareness to learn a good throwing motion until at least five, and some not until seven or eight. Until then just keep an eye out for flying Legos.

WHAT YOU NEED BEFORE YOU START

For young kids, I like to start with a tennis ball. They're cheap, easy to find, and about the right size and weight for little hands and arms. They also do minimal damage to windows and noses. I'd recommend rounding up several balls—it cuts down on the time spent running after stray throws.

The area you play in doesn't have to be particularly large—twenty or thirty feet in the longest dimension will do for a start. More important is to have some kind of backstop—a fence or a wall without windows—behind at least one end of the area, and preferably both. That way, you can play catch instead of fetch. If no other backstop is available, try hanging up a plastic tarp.

BASIC TECHNIQUE

Grip

Have your kid hold the ball with three fingers over the top, and the thumb underneath. Be sure the ball is held with the fingers and never touches the palm. This keeps the wrist loose and helps her let go of the ball at the right time.

Stance

Have her stand with her feet a little more than a shoulder's width apart, facing sideways to the direction she's throwing. Her throwing arm should be farthest away from the target. She should point the toe of her front foot directly at the target (see drawing).

Throw

The key to teaching a good throw is teaching it backward. By that I mean you teach the end of the motion first. Then you add the earlier steps one at a time until you work your way back to the start.

You do this because the whole first half of the motion is just preparation. That's why baseball pitchers have such wildly different windups. All they're doing is getting ready. But when they actually throw the ball, they all look pretty similar.

Step 1: The wrist snap

Once her feet are in the sideways stance described above, have your kid turn at the waist so the upper body is facing the target. She should hold the ball up in front of her so her arm looks like the letter L. Make sure the elbow is at shoulder height and the hand is pointing straight up.

Next, have her lay her wrist back, then snap it forward, releasing the ball toward the target. The ball won't go very far, but it should go in a straight line.

Step 2: The follow-through

After a few wrist snaps, add the forearm to your kid's motion. Start her out in the same L position, with the elbow high and the wrist back. This time, when she snaps her wrist forward to release the ball, have her straighten the elbow and finish with the arm and fingers pointing forward, directly at the target (see drawing). The ball should go a little farther this time, and it should still be on line.

Step 3. The turn

Up to this point we've been working with the part of the throw that gives accuracy. Now we're ready to add some power.

Get your kid into the same stance as before, but turn the upper body back to its natural position—facing sideways to the target. Raise the arm up and make another L, this time with the elbow pointing *away* from the target. Make sure the elbow is still as high as the shoulder. The forearm is pointing straight up, and the wrist is back.

Have her raise her nonthrowing arm in front of her for balance. It should be held in a comfortable position, with the wrist and forearm around shoulder level and the elbow pointing at the target (see drawing). Take the time to get this position right. She should look balanced and relaxed.

In slow motion, without actually throwing, have her turn toward the target, keeping the elbow high and the hand pointing straight up. As she finishes her turn, she should snap the arm and wrist forward just as she did before, pointing at the target on the follow-through. Repeat this several times, until it looks smooth and natural. Then try it at full speed and let her release the ball.

This time the ball should go considerably farther. At first the turn and the snap may seem like separate events. Slow them down again until it's one continuous motion from turn to snap. Once it looks smooth, try it at full speed.

Step 4. The step

Now comes the *real* power behind the throw. It's time for your kid to use her weight and the muscles in her legs.

Go back to the same starting position as in Step 3. Have her narrow her stance a little, to just under a shoulder's width. The body should still face sideways to the target.

In slow motion, have her step directly toward the target with the front foot, and push off with the back foot. As her weight moves forward, she should turn her body and follow through just like before. When she finishes, her weight should be on the front leg, and that knee should be bent (see drawing). The arm and fingers should be pointing at the target.

Again, do this a bunch of times, going slowly until the motion looks natural and smooth. The sequence of movements is very important:

first step, then turn as the weight comes forward, then snap the wrist into the follow-through. Make sure the front knee is bent so the weight can shift all the way onto that leg.

Congratulations! You've just taught your kid to throw!

Step 5. The windup

I'd recommend using as little windup as possible, or none at all, until the motion looks completely natural and smooth. But here's a simple windup that's fluid and easy, when you think your kid is ready.

Start her facing sideways to the target, with the hands together at about belly-button height and the feet less than a shoulder's width apart. As she steps forward, her hands should drop down past her thighs and spread out like wings on either side. The idea is to let them swing naturally into the same position they were in at the beginning of Step 3. Her arms spread out and she steps toward the target at the same time. Now her weight comes forward, and she turns and throws, just like before.

Step 6. Practice

As you've figured out by now, this is a complicated motion. No one gets it on the first try. Let your kid take plenty of time to get comfortable with each step, and expect some confusion every time you add something new. When that happens, don't be afraid to go back and reconstruct the motion from the beginning. Retreating to familiar ground will rebuild her confidence and keep her from feeling overwhelmed.

Once the basic motion is learned, it becomes natural only through repetition. The more she throws, the better she'll get. Of course, it's hard to do a lot of throwing unless both of you know how to catch. We'll cover that in the next chapter.

TROUBLESHOOTING

There are lots of things that can go wrong with a throw. Luckily, most problems are easy to diagnose and fix. Here are the most common ones:

The Shot Put

If your kid seems to be pushing the ball instead of throwing it, check the position of the arm before she makes her throw. The elbow of the throwing arm should be up at shoulder level and pointing away from the target, not down at the ground. Her hand should point straight up or a little backward, not cocked forward next to the ear. As she throws, make sure the elbow stays *high.*

The Strobe Effect

When you learn something one step at a time, it's hard to put all the pieces together. If your kid looks like she's moving through a series of still-life poses, that's what's happening. The secret here is to slow down the process. Work on the transitions between the steps, and take them one at a time. Do it in slow motion until the transition is continuous and smooth. Then speed it up little by little, until it looks smooth at normal speeds.

Wild Throws

You can usually tell why a throw is off target by where the ball goes.

• If the throws are too high, your child is probably not following through. Remind her to snap the wrist and point at the target when she's done.

• Low throws happen when a kid bends over too far as she finishes the throw. Have her keep the body a little more upright and bend the front knee instead. Also, check her grip. If she's holding the ball with the palm instead of the fingers, she might have trouble letting go at the right time.

• If a right-handed thrower keeps missing to the right, the ball may be slipping out of her hand. Remind her to get a good grip on the ball and make sure she follows through, pointing at the target. The other possibility is that she's letting the hand drop and throwing the ball from the side. Make sure the elbow stays higher than her shoulder and keep her forearm pointing straight up.

• If a right-handed thrower misses to the left, she may be stepping in that direction. Make sure she steps directly toward the target. This is easier to remember if she steps before she starts her turn.

Weak Throws

The power behind a throw comes from the forward movement of your child's weight, and then the turning of her upper body. If her throws don't have much *oomph,* make sure she's taking a good, healthy step— at least a half shoulder-width long. She should finish with her weight over the front leg, and the front knee should be bent to accept the weight.

Once she's taking a good step, check her turn. Make sure she starts the motion facing sideways, with the throwing elbow pointing away from the target. You can emphasize this by having her turn a little bit *past* sideways. Tell her to "show some buns" before she steps. It'll crack her up, and it'll also keep her from turning too soon.

It's important to step first, *then* turn. That lets the force from the legs travel through the upper body and into the arm.

SAFETY TIPS

Obviously there are some safety issues when you teach a kid to send projectiles flying through the air. We'll cover most of those in *Chapter 3: Catch a Ball.* But the act of throwing comes with risks of its own.

Before throwing, you and your child should warm up thoroughly.

Swing your arms from the shoulders in different-sized circles, first in one direction and then the other. Never throw hard before you're warmed up. Start with a slow, easy motion and a short distance, then throw longer and harder as your muscles get loose.

Children should never throw sidearm. It places too much strain on the elbow. The same goes for curveballs. Unless you're pitching competitively at the high school level or above, you'll never need anything but an overhand fastball. Also, be careful when you trade the tennis ball for something heavier. Take it easy, and quit as soon as anyone's arm gets tired.

By the way, all of this goes double for grown-ups. Believe me, you're not as young as you used to be, and neither are your joints. If you give yourself bursitis or tendonitis, who's going to play catch with your kid?

WHAT'S NEXT

Throwing is a useful skill all by itself. It will serve your kids well, whether they're defending themselves in a neighborhood snowball fight or just skipping stones. However, the finest expression of the art of throwing is in the sport of baseball. There are baseball leagues available for boys and girls of all ages and skills. And through adult softball leagues, it's a game that some people play their entire lives.

RECORD THROWS

• The fastest pitch ever measured with reliable equipment traveled at 101 miles an hour. It was thrown by Nolan Ryan on August 20, 1974 *(Guinness World Records)*.

• The longest throw by a woman was 296 feet, thrown by Mildred "Babe" Didrickson on July 25, 1931 *(Guinness World Records)*.

BEGINNER'S ARM

If you've been throwing all your life, it probably seems automatic—as natural as falling off a log. That makes it hard for you to understand how slowly you should teach this skill. Luckily, there's a way for you to turn back the clock and become a beginner again. Just follow the same steps as your kid, going through each one as she does—but use your other arm.

You'll be amazed how difficult and complicated this "natural" motion suddenly feels. Immediately, you'll understand the complexity of what your kid is doing, and how you can help her. As an added bonus, you'll both get a good laugh out of it, and your child will feel less incompetent and less intimidated as she sees you struggling right by her side.

THE PHYSICS OF THROWING

When you throw, you take the strength of the big muscles in the middle of your body and use it to increase the speed of your arm and hand. In this way, your body acts like a lever. A lever is a stick that rotates around a point called a fulcrum, just like your arm rotates around the center of your body. The parts of the stick closest to the fulcrum can generate force, but the parts farthest from the fulcrum move at greater speed.

Try this. Take a fork with a flat handle and place it on the table so the pointy end curves upward. Place a penny on the middle of the handle. Tell your kid to push down the pointy end of the fork and notice how high the penny goes. Now put the penny on the very end of the handle. Have her push down on the other end with the same amount of force as before. This time the penny will go much higher.

This is why you want her to keep the elbow and hand away from her body when she throws. That makes her arm into a longer lever, and a longer lever gives her a faster throw.

TARGET PRACTICE

Kids are always trying to throw fast, but it's much harder to get them to throw accurately. The best way around this is to set up a little target practice.

Place a sawhorse in front of a fence or a wall that can serve as a backstop. If you don't have a sawhorse, a plank between two chairs works fine. Fill some tin cans with rocks or some plastic bottles with water, and set them up as targets. You want something heavy enough so it takes a direct hit to knock it over.

Have your kids stand far enough away so they can reach the targets with a good strong throw. Then hand them a ball and watch what happens. After one round you'll be begging them to let you have a turn.

STUPID THROWING JOKES

Q: What do butterflies use to play catch?
A: Mothballs.

Q: Why is baseball so cool?
A: Because of all the fans.

Q: How come you shouldn't play baseball on the African savanna?
A: Too many *cheetahs*.

3
CATCH A BALL

"Hey... Dad?... You wanna have a catch?"
—*Ray Kinsella, in the film* Field of Dreams

I t's a simple game. Two people stand a few paces apart and send a ball back and forth in a low, graceful arc. Sometimes they talk. Sometimes they don't. But always there's the smack of leather against leather—slow and steady, like a heartbeat.

When I was a kid, we used to vacation every year on Cape Cod with the same family. They had four boys, just like we did, and one of them was my best friend. His name was Mark.

When you see your best friend just once a year it's not the same as if he went to your school or lived in your neighborhood. Every time you get together, there's a hesitation. What if one of you has changed? What if he's not the way you remembered him? What if he doesn't even like you anymore? But there's also a sense of urgency. This is the only chance we have to see each other! We don't have much time! We have to start having fun right away!

Mark and I had a ritual the first time we got together each year. As our car rolled up to the rental cottage, almost before we came to a stop, I'd pull on my baseball mitt and jump out. Mark would be waiting there with his mitt on, and he'd whip a fastball right at me as I got out of the car. *THWACK*—the ball would smack into my glove. Before we unpacked our stuff, or begged our moms for a snack, or started thinking up ways to harass our brothers, we'd always play catch. And after a little while, we'd remember why we were friends.

By the end of the week we were inseparable again. At the end of each day, our mothers would plead with us to come inside while we flung a ball back and forth in light too dim for grown-ups' eyes. And on the day we had to leave, after all our stuff was packed and everyone else was ready to go, my dad would have to yell at me so I'd stop playing catch and get in the car. As we backed out the driveway, I'd lean out the window and hold up my mitt. There was always just enough time for one or two more throws.

I lost touch with Mark years ago. Nowadays I play catch with my daughter instead. We go out after dinner and throw until it's too dark to see—or until my wife sticks her head out the door and yells for us to come inside.

WHEN TO START

Learning to catch takes coordination and a willingness to overcome one's fears. Most kids are ready to try it by age seven, and some by age five.

A lot of kids learn to catch after they learn to throw. Catching is simpler mechanically, but it's more difficult for most kids to learn, because of the fear factor. Once they learn to throw, there's more incentive because it's hard to practice throwing unless they know how to catch.

WHAT YOU NEED BEFORE YOU START

A Glove

Even a perfect glove won't catch the ball for you, but a bad one will make you drop it every time. Here are a few things to consider when you buy a glove for your child.

• *Size*. A glove is measured from the top of its webbing—between the thumb and forefinger—to its "heel," down where the hand goes in. Most six-year-olds can handle a nine-inch glove. Much smaller than that and it's hard to catch a standard-sized baseball. How quickly the glove size increases depends on how quickly your kid grows. By the time he hits his growth spurt, he can use an adult size—about twelve inches. At any age, the glove should be small enough so it stays on the hand, so he can move it around easily, and so he can open and close it.

• *Flexibility*. This is a crucial factor in your child's success. If the glove is too stiff to open and close, he'll never catch anything. Synthetic gloves are the least expensive, and are sometimes more supple in the beginning. Leather, however, will last longer and will be more pliable after you break it in. Whichever you choose, buy the most flexible one you can find and break it in well (see below). For this reason, a well-worn hand-me-down glove may be the best choice of all.

• *Shape*. First of all, choose a standard fielder's glove. If your kid ends up as a catcher or a first baseman, he can invest in a specialty glove then, but everyone needs a fielder's glove.

Eventually, when the mitt is broken in, you want it to open and close almost as if it were hinged, and to lie flat when you put it down. The closer you are to this shape from the start, the easier it is to achieve. Avoid stiff gloves that lie wide-open, like a basket. Catching a ball with one of these is like catching a ball with a mixing bowl.

Balls

I mean that literally, not figuratively. A few tennis balls should do the trick—they're easy to throw and they don't do any damage. Most kids are familiar with them and know they won't get hurt if they get bonked with one. You might also want to invest in a soft practice ball. These are the size and weight of a baseball, but much softer. They're a nice transition to the real thing, and their extra weight is easier to feel when it hits the glove.

A Place to Play Catch

Nothing too fancy needed here. Locate about twenty feet of clear space, and a wall or a fence at one end to serve as a backstop.

BASIC TECHNIQUE

Let's start with the basics. Kids aren't stupid. When something comes flying through the air at them, their instincts (reinforced by millions of years of collective human experience) tell them to get the heck out of the way. Everything we're about to do is designed to extinguish that impulse—and replace it with another. We want to convince them that they aren't under attack. We want them to act like predators instead of prey.

With that said, almost every kid reverts to prey mode at some point. When that happens, flip ahead to the troubleshooting tips. There should be something there to get him back on track.

Step 1: The basic catch

Have your child stand about five feet away from you with his non-throwing hand raised to chest level. He should hold his hand a comfortable distance in front of him, with the elbow bent. His wrist should be laid back a little so that the palm faces you, and his thumb should be more or less parallel to the ground.

With a gentle, underhand motion, toss a tennis ball so it reaches his hand near the top of its arc. Have him watch the ball all the way in and catch it with one hand. This may take longer to master than you'd think, but it's a crucial first step. Just take your time and dole out lavish praise for anything that even approaches success. At some point, he'll suddenly get it.

Once he has the timing down and can catch the ball at least half the time, have him put on a mitt. Keep tossing until he gets used to the weight and feel of it. Tell him to watch the ball all the way into the mitt, and to squeeze it once it arrives. If the mitt is a little stiff, he can place the other hand behind it to help him squeeze.

As he starts making catches more consistently, move him back to a distance of about ten feet. Now your tosses will still be underhand, but they'll need to be a little faster, or they'll have too much arc. Try to put the ball right in his mitt, so he doesn't have to reach for it.

Step 2: Moving to the ball

Now your child can catch a ball if it's coming right to him. This is an accomplishment, but it's only the first step. What if the ball isn't thrown directly at his mitt? This requires some adjustments. The first adjustment is to teach him to move his body toward the ball.

You'll start by having him move toward the ball even when it's coming right at him. Toss the ball to his mitt, just as before, but tell him to step forward with the foot on the same side as his catching hand. As he steps, his body weight should shift onto that foot, and his head and shoulders should come forward as well.

You don't want him to lift his foot high off the ground and stamp

it. Get him to use a smooth motion that doesn't jar his body. Also, make sure he isn't reaching out and snapping at the ball. The arm should stay relaxed and the elbow a little bent. This is a movement of the body, not the hand. You want him to meet the ball—not swat at it or passively wait for it (see drawing).

Once he's moving forward to meet each throw, start tossing the ball a little to the side. He should still be stepping forward, but also angling toward the throw. If the ball comes in low, have him bend his knees to get down to it. No matter where the throw is, his mitt, the foot on his mitt side, and his head should all move to meet it.

Step 3: Glove position

When a throw is more than a little off line, simply moving toward it isn't enough. You have to reach for it too. And depending on where you're reaching, you hold your mitt in a different position.

Have your child stand with the mitt in front of his chest in the catching position. The elbow is bent, and the wrist is laid back so his palm faces you. Have him sweep his arm up and out in a circle, like the second hand of a clock, then down until it points at the ground between his feet. Have him sweep back through the circle, past the original starting point, until the mitt points down toward the foot on the opposite side. His palm should face forward throughout this arc (see drawing).

Now toss the ball to each position on the circle in turn. Make sure he holds his glove as he did when he swept around the circle. If a ball goes toward his elbow, at the center of the circle, he should hold his mitt up in the "twelve o'clock" position and bend his knees to get down to it. Now have him step toward the ball again, just like before. Make him reach a little farther to catch each throw. With each catch, check for correct mitt position, and make sure he steps forward to meet the ball.

TROUBLESHOOTING

The Fear Factor

This is by far the most common problem you'll face with beginners. It can show up in a number of ways.

If your child is flinching with every throw, go back to a softer ball and a shorter toss. Use a foam ball if necessary. Once he gets comfortable, try the tennis ball again and add distance slowly.

Another fear response is the backward lean. This one is harder to correct. Initially, just remind him to step toward the ball and lean his head and shoulders forward. If that doesn't work, find a baseball cap with an adjustable loop in back and put it on his head backward. Tie a string from the loop to the back of his mitt. Make it just long enough so it goes tight when the mitt is in catching position. Now have him try to catch the ball without pulling his cap off. The head has to follow the mitt, which keeps him from leaning back.

The last fear reflex is the step-back. Your child may still be able to catch a ball while stepping backward, but it will look awkward and defensive. Place a long stick on the ground directly behind his heels and ask him to catch the ball without stepping on the stick. Often, that's enough to make him aware of his feet and keep him from stepping back.

Lunging, Swatting, Snapping

Rather than receiving the ball with soft hands, some kids will flail away at it and try to snap or swat it out of the air with their mitts. This is a problem of too much arm motion and not enough body. Remind him to keep his wrist laid back so the palm faces the thrower. Have him keep his elbow bent. Then make sure he meets the ball by stepping toward it rather than reaching.

Basket Catching

Some kids try to catch every ball by turning their palm skyward and hoping the ball will drop into it as if it were a basket. This works fine for high, arcing tosses that fall more or less straight down. However, as soon as you throw them a ball that moves in a straighter line, it rolls up their arm and hits them square in the chest. This is to be avoided.

The key here is to remind them of the proper mitt position, and give them throws that move more horizontally than vertically. Even soft tosses can be made horizontal by standing close enough so the throw hits the top of its arc just before it reaches their mitt.

Eyes Off the Ball

Sometimes this is a variant on flinching, and sometimes it's just a failure to watch the ball. Whatever the cause, he'll never catch what he can't see. Here's a game that will force him to track the ball with his eyes.

Take two identical tennis balls and mark one of them with a small red circle. Hide both balls behind your back, or in your mitt. Now throw one of them to your kid. See if he can catch the ball and tell you if it was the marked ball or the blank one. When this gets too easy, mark the other ball with a red square. Most kids get so absorbed in trying to see which ball you threw, they don't even notice that they're catching every one.

No Squeeze

Usually this is simply a stiff mitt. In the short run, just have the child use the other hand to help squeeze the ball. As soon as you can, work in the mitt so it's pliable enough to open and close with one hand (see "Breaking in a mitt," below).

WHAT'S NEXT

Pop-ups

There's nothing more satisfying than tracking a high fly ball against a cobalt sky until it plunges earthward and comes to rest in the pocket of your mitt. Unfortunately, it's also a good way to get a black eye or lose some teeth.

Start with a tennis ball and make your throws low and easy at first. Have your kids move quickly beneath the ball, rather than drifting and leaning. Tell them not to straighten their arms—bent elbows make it much easier to adjust at the last second. And above all, tell them to watch the ball!

Grounders

Here's another place where the fear factor is high. Practice grounders where there's a smooth, even surface. Bad hops mean lots of bruises.

Throw the ball so it reaches them on the third or fourth hop. Tell them to bend the knees, get the butt down, and get the mitt down. They should watch the ball all the way into the mitt, and use both hands—with the bare hand coming down from above, like an alligator's upper jaw—to gather the ball in.

Once they're fielding the ball cleanly, try throwing the ball off to the side. They need to sidestep like a crab and get in front of the ball, then scoop it up the same way they did before.

SAFETY TIPS

All of this is just common sense, but it's worth reviewing with your child. Before he throws, he needs to make eye contact with the person he's throwing to. He should also make sure the area is clear of other people, and that there's nothing breakable within range of even the wildest of throws. Finally, he should never throw anything unless the person he's throwing to is confident about catching it.

BREAKING IN A MITT

For some people, a baseball mitt is more than a piece of equipment—it's a treasured possession, almost like a pet. No wonder people take so much time and care breaking in a new one. Unfortunately, there's little agreement on the best way to do it.

The time-tested method is to keep on playing until the mitt loses its stiffness. Unfortunately, this can take a long time. Most people try to hasten the process by using some kind of oil or grease. I've heard of everything from shaving cream to cooking oil to Vaseline. But whatever you use, don't oil the mitt unless you're sure it's made of real leather. A synthetic mitt won't absorb the oil, and you'll be left with a horrible, sticky mess. Here's the method I use. I don't know that it's the best, but it works.

Buy a small bottle of unscented mineral oil at the drugstore. Unlike vegetable oil, it won't go rancid. Some sporting goods stores sell "mitt oil," but it's mostly just mineral oil. Put a very small amount in the pocket of the glove and work it in with your fingers. Remember that the pocket is the area just below the webbing, not the webbing itself. Once the oil is absorbed, add a little more and work it in again. Apply the oil mainly to the pocket and down the crease of the glove to the heel, where you want it to bend. A very thin coat to the rest of the glove will keep the leather from drying out, but too much oil adds unnecessary weight to the glove.

Once the pocket and the crease areas have taken all the oil they can absorb, put an old baseball in the pocket of the mitt and wrap a belt around it. Make sure it's folded exactly the way you want it to be when it's broken in. Then put it under a mattress and leave it overnight. Repeat this every night, using the mitt often during the day to make sure it gets opened and closed as much as possible. Once it's pliable enough to open and close easily with one hand, you're done.

ZEN AND THE ART OF GLOVE MAKING

Some people say that baseball is almost a religion in Japan. Well, at the very least it's an art form. There's a man there named Yoshi Tsubota who has made baseball gloves for more than fifty years. Recently, he was designated a Master Craftsman and a national treasure by the Emperor of Japan—an honor roughly equivalent to being knighted in England. He has created gloves for some of the best baseball players in the world. Each glove is worth thousands of dollars, and fits its owner exactly in size, shape, and degree of suppleness.

GAMES

Although I've always preferred a plain old game of catch, there are ways to spice it up for a change of pace. Try counting how many consecutive catches you can make without a drop. You can also try stepping back after each throw to see how far apart the two of you get before someone drops the ball. And then there's the time-honored game known as "pickle."

Two players stand about twenty to forty feet apart beside objects that are designated as bases. A runner starts out standing on a base, and the two players begin to play catch. The object is for the runner to go back and forth between the bases as many times as he can without being tagged. A player can tag the runner only if he is holding the ball, and if the runner is not touching the base.

STUPID CATCHING JOKES

Q: What did the glove say when the ball flew by?
A: Catch ya later!

Q: What is it that everyone can catch but no one can throw?
A: A cold.

Q: How come the catcher didn't dance with Cinderella?
A: He missed the ball.

4
PLANT A TREE

"A civilization flourishes when people plant trees under whose shade they will never sit."

—Greek proverb

When I was a kid, we had a little blue spruce tree in our yard. It was my favorite. I loved its thick, silvery needles and the way it reminded me of Christmas even on a summer day.

One December someone cut it down in the middle of the night and hauled it away. It was probably some kids from the local college looking to decorate their dorm room. I say this because they left behind a hammer, an unlikely choice of instruments for professional tree-nappers. My father liked the hammer and considered it a fair trade, but I was heartbroken.

I pestered my dad for months until he finally agreed to replace it with another tree. But rather than buy one at a nursery, we drove out to some nearby woods to dig one up. At first we tried to get one as big as the missing spruce, but the root ball was too heavy to lift. Instead, we ended up with a scrawny little pine tree that barely came up to my waist. I was disappointed, to say the least. We planted it without much fanfare and it was soon forgotten.

Many years after my parents had moved from that house, I went back for a visit. No one was home, so I couldn't look inside, but I took a minute to wander around the yard. A lot of things had changed—

whole garden beds had been moved, and new plantings were every-where. So when I came to the little pine tree, it took me a while to rec-ognize it.

It was well over twenty feet tall. Its trunk was as thick as my leg. Years of fallen needles had laid a deep, soft carpet at its feet.

When you plant a tree, the fruits of your labor take a long time to appear. That's why you should also try to harvest something less tangible—like hope, or faith. For those things, you don't have to wait. As soon as your tree is planted, you can lean on your shovel, wipe the sweat from your brow, and imagine your grandchildren playing in its shade.

WHEN TO START

Tree planting is a great activity to do with kids. It requires no special skills or dexterity, and it can be done at a leisurely pace. Better yet, it involves lots of dirt and water and being outside. You can include your kids as soon as they're old enough to understand what you're doing—somewhere around age three or four.

Little ones can help break up soil clods, spread mulch and bone meal, and pour water. Just keep an eye on them to make sure they don't grab at the limbs or roots of a delicate young tree. If they're a little older, they can help decide which tree to plant and take a bigger part in the planting.

WHAT YOU NEED BEFORE YOU START

A Good Place to Plant

This is the most important thing you'll need to find. Although you can grow some type of tree in almost any spot, the location will determine what your choices are. Here are some things to consider:

• *Space*. How much room will your tree have? Not just at first, but ten or twenty years from now. Are there overhead wires or eaves? Would a tree scrape against your house, or drop fruit or leaves on your garage? And remember, it won't just grow up and out, but down as well. Would its roots buckle your driveway, crack your foundation, or invade your sewer lines?

If you aren't sure about the location of your underground utilities, call up the utility company. They're usually more than happy to help prevent damage to their lines from root invasion or overzealous digging.

• *Soil*. Different trees like different dirt. Most do best in rich, moist, well-drained soil, but that kind of perfection is rare. When you're considering a spot for planting, dig a little test hole to see what you've got. Some soil is sandy; some is dense as clay. Some spots are moist year-round, while others can get as dry as bone. Knowing your soil will help you pick the right tree for your location.

• *Sun*. How many hours a day will your tree get full sunlight? Will this change when the sun travels a lower arc in the winter? If the spot is in shade, is it a dense shade or is there filtered light through overhead branches?

• *Wind*. Are there strong winds that could break young branches or topple a shallow-rooted tree?

• *Water*. Do dense foliage or overhanging eaves block the rain? Is the spot within reach of a garden hose from an outdoor spigot?

• **_Surrounding plants_**. If there are other large plantings nearby, your tree may have to compete for root space and nutrition. And as time passes, the tree will grow, casting new shadows that could shade existing gardens.

Make a few notes about your possible planting locations and bring them with you when you go to buy a tree. Putting the right tree in the right spot is the best guarantee of success.

Tools

You'll need only a few tools, but try to get good ones. They'll make your work easier, and they'll last for years.

The most important tool for planting is a good spade. It should have a long, sturdy handle to pry up heavy soils and reach to the bottom of holes. A garden rake is also useful for spreading and mixing soil. Both of these can be found in smaller kids' versions, and for little kids, it's nice to have some. Kids feel much more involved when they get to dig in the dirt and move it around, even if they aren't moving very much at a time.

Another great tool for digging is a gouging bar, or "rock breaker." It's a long, heavy, iron bar with a wedge at one end for breaking up rocks or compacted soil. It's also great for cutting through big roots or levering up big rocks. Even relatively soft ground can be difficult for a child to dig in. If you use a gouging bar to break it up first, the task becomes much easier.

Finally, some sharp pruning shears will come in handy for trimming branches and roots.

Water

It takes a lot of water to plant and grow a tree. Unless you're planting in a swamp or willing to haul a lot of water by hand, your spot should be within hose reach of a spigot.

Soil Amendments

This is a controversial subject. The traditional approach is to improve the soil around a new tree with organic material. This ensures good drainage and moisture retention, and makes it easy for new roots to penetrate and grow. However, some people advocate refilling the hole with only the original soil. They claim soil amendments cause the roots to stay in "good" soil, rather than spreading outward.

I've always amended the soil when I plant a tree, with good success. I've also seen young trees die in bad soil because they couldn't get a decent start. If your soil is already good, amendments are probably unnecessary. But in most cases I'd lean toward improving the soil.

Almost any kind of decomposed organic material will do. Compost is probably the best, but well-rotted leaves are easier to find, and they work great. Manure improves the soil and adds nutrition at the same time. But beware of fresh manure, which can burn sensitive roots, and cattle manure, which contains a lot of soluble salts that damage certain trees.

One easily available amendment is peat moss. It does great things for soil texture, but it makes soil acidic. Some trees like that, but some definitely don't. If necessary, the acid can be neutralized with lime. Check with the nursery about this when you buy the tree.

Mulch

Mulch is anything you spread on top of the soil to control erosion, water loss, weed growth, and root damage from heat or cold. It can be in-
organic, like black plastic or gravel, or organic, like bark, straw, grass
clippings, or leaves.

I prefer organic mulches, because they eventually break down to
enrich the soil, and because they let water and air pass through to the
soil and roots. Their one disadvantage is that they need to be replen-
ished every year.

Get enough mulch to cover a circle about twice as wide as the initial branch spread of your tree, to a depth of about three or four inches.

Extras

The most dangerous time in a young tree's life is the first year after
planting. This is when it is most vulnerable to drought, damage, and
disease. What allows a tree to thrive during this crucial time is a good,
strong root system.

Many factors are involved in getting a root system established. Careful handling of the tree, good soil preparation, and the right amount of
water all come into play. At the time of planting, there are a couple of
other things you can add that might give your tree a head start.

The three nutrients that all plants need are nitrogen, phosphorus,
and potassium. Nitrogen promotes leafy growth, and potassium helps
with fruiting, but it's phosphorus that makes the biggest difference in
the growth of new roots. An excellent natural source of phosphorus is
bone meal. You can find it at any garden store, but buy the small box.
You need only a handful or two to plant a tree.

The other substance used at planting time is vitamin B_1. It is re-
puted to promote root growth and lessen the shock of being trans-

planted. I've talked to some old-timers who think it's a lot of hooey, but others swear by it, and it's coming into more and more common use.

BASIC TECHNIQUE

Step 1: Timing

Certain times of year are better than others for planting trees. Obviously, the ground can't be frozen solid. And if you plant in the middle of the summer, you're going to have to do a lot of watering to make sure those tender roots don't dry out. In general, fall and spring are the best planting seasons.

In the spring, there's a larger selection of trees, and they may be less expensive. You also have a full growing season before the deep chill of winter. But if you live where winter temperatures rarely sink below freezing, fall is also a great time to plant. New roots can grow throughout a mild, wet winter, and the tree will be well established by the time it faces the stress of summer heat.

If you're planting during a rainy season, make sure you aren't digging up soil that's soaking wet. Muddy soil loses all its air when you work with it, and it may smother the roots. Dig your hole when it hasn't rained for a few days, and keep the soil dry under a tarp until you're ready to plant.

Step 2: Choosing a tree

There are many times in life when it pays to shop around for the lowest price. This is not one of those times. Mail order trees are small and often of poor quality. Plant sections at giant home centers are not much better. And when you transplant a wild tree, you risk serious damage to the tree and your back before you're done.

For a few extra dollars it's more than worth it to buy a tree at a reputable nursery. The selection of trees, their health and quality, and the expert help you'll receive can't be duplicated in any other setting.

Set aside several hours when you go to buy a tree. You'll want plenty of time to wander around, ask advice, and make your selection. Bring your notes about your intended planting site to discuss with the nursery staff. And above all, bring your kids. They'll love the rows and rows of exotic plants, and helping select the tree will give them a sense of involvement and ownership right from the start.

TYPES OF TREES

This is where knowing your planting site is crucial. How tall do you want your tree to be? How wide? A deciduous tree might provide shade in summer, bright colors in autumn, and sunshine through its bare branches in winter. It also might drop a ton of leaves all over your driveway.

What shape do you want? Do you want fruit? Pretty leaves? Interesting bark? Flowers? Berries? A lovely scent? How fast do you want it to grow? How long do you want it to live? How much energy do you want to put into pruning, watering, fertilizing, and pest control?

If you have strong preferences on any of these issues, the time to voice them is before you buy. This is why you're buying a tree at a nursery. The staff will help you find the right tree to fit your location and needs.

PACKAGING

Young trees are packaged for sale in one of three ways.

Bare root trees arrive in the nurseries in late winter or early spring. These are young, deciduous trees that were removed from the ground after they dropped their leaves and became dormant. They are missing most of their small feeder roots, and their main roots are usually packed in wood shavings or some other moist material.

Though they may look like lifeless sticks, bare root trees have many advantages. Because they're easier to ship, they're a lot less expensive, and they arrive at the nurseries in great variety and large numbers. They're also easier to fit in a car and carry to a planting site. Their main drawbacks are that they are available for only a few months of the year and their exposed roots require special care during and after planting.

Some trees, like evergreens, don't have a dormant season when they can survive in bare root form. For these trees, the whole root ball is dug up and wrapped in burlap, or some other material. Ball-and-burlap trees are available in cooler months, when the root ball is in less danger of drying out. They are better protected than bare root trees, but often more expensive and more difficult to transport.

The other way to purchase a tree is in a container. It may have grown that way all its life, or it may have been a bare root tree that was moved to a container at the end of its dormant phase. This form is the most expensive, but it lets you plant a tree any time of year, including the autumn planting season that many people prefer.

HEALTH

Once you've decided what kind of tree to buy, make sure you pick a healthy specimen that will get off to a good start. Examine every part of the tree in turn.

Does the tree have a good shape? Branches that come off the main trunk at less than a 45-degree angle will be weak and prone to breakage. Trunks that divide into more than one lead branch may develop a weak crotch and split apart. Some lopsidedness can be corrected with pruning, but choosing a nicely shaped tree from the start is usually better.

Examine the bark for splits or damage. Look for broken branches. Are the leaves or needles uniform in shape and color? Have they been nibbled by pests or stunted by disease?

The most important part of the tree is its root system. Bare root trees should have plump, well-developed roots with no evidence of damage or drying. Ball-and-burlap trees should have a firm, moist root ball without exposed roots at the top. If a container tree has surface roots circling around the trunk or good-sized roots poking out of the drain holes at the bottom, it may be root-bound. When main roots are forced to spiral around the inside of a container, they may never straighten out. In time they can choke each other off and kill the tree.

Step 3: Preparing the tree

When you put the tree in your car and transport it home, try not to bend branches or damage tender bark, and be especially careful with bare or burlapped roots. Once you get home, your preparation will depend on the way your tree is packaged.

If your bare root tree is still packed in wood shavings, make sure they remain moist. If the roots are exposed, lay the tree on its side with the roots in a shallow trench. Cover the roots with soil and water them well. The tree will keep this way for a few days, but the sooner you plant it, the better. A couple of hours before you're ready to plant, fill a large basin or garbage can with water and soak the roots. Don't leave them soaking for days—roots need air to survive.

Ball-and-burlap root balls need to stay moist. If you won't be planting for a couple of days, water lightly and wrap the ball in plastic to prevent evaporation. Water again the day before planting.

Containers should be kept moist and watered thoroughly the day before planting.

Step 4: Digging a hole

There's an old saying: "Buy a one dollar plant—dig a twenty dollar hole." The hole you dig will determine how well the tree's roots grow, and that will determine your success.

Start by clearing the turf and weeds from a circle of ground four or five times the diameter of your root ball. At the center of this area dig a hole two or three times as wide as the root ball, and a little less deep than the roots are long. Put the topsoil in one pile and the dense or rocky undersoil in a different pile. Around the bottom of the hole, dig about six inches deeper, leaving a platform of firm soil in the middle.

If your kids are old enough to handle a shovel, you can break up the ground for them with the gouging bar and they can remove the soil. The gouging bar will also help if you run into roots or rocks along the way.

Once your hole is big enough, make sure its sides are rough, not smooth. This will help young roots penetrate into the surrounding soil.

If you're using compost, peat moss, or manure to amend the soil, mix it with the topsoil, using one part amendment to at least three parts dirt. You can also add a couple cups of bone meal if you like.

Step 5: Planting the tree

The cardinal sin of tree planting is planting too deep. The thickened area just above where the roots come together is called the crown, and if it gets buried, the tree will be susceptible to fungal infection and rot. The goal is to plant the tree with its usual soil line slightly higher than the new surrounding soil. That way, even if the ground beneath it settles, the crown stays high and dry.

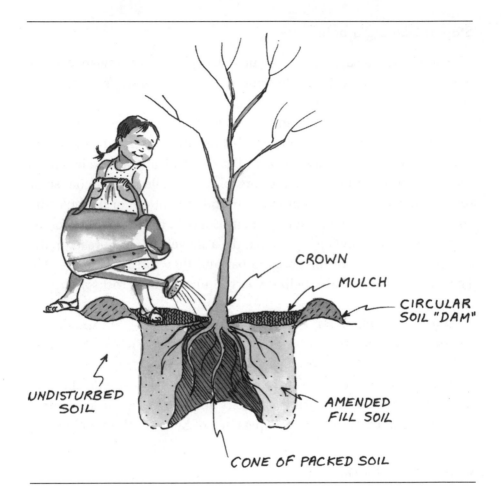

CROWN

MULCH

CIRCULAR
SOIL "DAM"

UNDISTURBED
SOIL

AMENDED
FILL SOIL

CONE OF PACKED SOIL

BARE ROOT TREES

Examine the root system and trim off any broken or dried-up ends. At the center of the hole, make a firm cone of soil to support the roots. Hold the tree in the hole and spread the roots around the cone. Place a stick or shovel handle across the hole to determine the soil line, and make sure the crown is a couple of inches above that level, adjusting the size of the cone as needed (see drawing).

Once you're happy with the depth, one of you should hold it while the other sights from several angles to make sure it's straight. You can mark the trunk position on the stick that you've placed across the hole, in case the tree tilts during planting. While one of you holds the tree in place, the other should start filling in the hole with amended soil.

Pat down the soil around the roots as you go. Once the hole is half filled, water thoroughly to get out any big air spaces. Fill the hole to the top and water again. Check to make sure the crown is still an inch or two above soil level. If it has settled too much, water well and gently pull the tree up to the correct level. At the edge of the hole, mound up the soil into a circular dam that will keep water from running away from the tree (see drawing).

Spread mulch around the tree, but keep it away from the base of the trunk. Water thoroughly, adding vitamin B_1 according to the directions if you like. Stakes and extra supports are not necessary unless the tree is exposed to heavy winds. The tree will be stronger if it stands up on its own.

Most bare root trees do better if you prune them at planting time. This allows them to put more energy into replacing their missing feeder roots, and less into growing leaves and branches. Start by removing any broken branches or ones that come off the tree at angles less than 45 degrees. You should also trim back any extra lead branches, leaving just one for upward growth. Finally, cut back all remaining branches by about one-fourth their length, pruning just above a healthy bud.

BALL-AND-BURLAP TREES

Without unwrapping the root ball, place it at the center of the hole and put a stick across the hole to mark the soil level. The top of the ball should be a couple of inches above the level of the surrounding soil. Sight from different angles to make sure the tree is straight, then fill the hole enough to cover the bottom third of the root ball with amended soil. Water thoroughly.

Next, unwrap the top two thirds of the ball and cut away the loose burlap. Fill in the rest of the hole, making sure that no burlap pokes through to the surface, where it can draw moisture away from the roots and into the air. Make a dam around the hole, water thoroughly, and mulch as described above for bare root trees. Prune dead or damaged branches only.

CONTAINER PLANTS

While the tree is still in its container, check the depth of the hole as you did for ball-and-burlap trees. Once the depth is right, cut away or gently remove the container. If the roots at the edge of the root ball have been crowded together, use a hose to spray away the outer layer of dirt and spread the roots away from the ball.

Plant as described above for ball-and-burlap trees.

Step 6: Taking care of it

If you've chosen the right tree for the right spot, it will eventually thrive all by itself. However, the first year after planting, the tree is in its weakest state. Here's what you can do to get it off to a good start:

• *Water.* The first few months, watering will be crucial. The soil should always feel moist beneath the mulch. When it dries out, water deeply and thoroughly to reach the lowest roots. If you like, you can water by hand and add vitamin B_1 for a few weeks. Kids love hand-watering new trees—it's like feeding a baby. But eventually you may want to switch to a drip watering system, or a soaker hose and a timer. Remember, though, the ground should be moist, not swampy. Over-watering will kill a tree just as surely as drought.

• *Fertilizer*. If you have planted in rich, fertile soil, fertilizer is probably not necessary. Too many nutrients can cause excessive growth before the root system is able to support it. But in sparse soil, a little feeding just before the flush of growth in the spring may be a good idea. Spread some balanced fertilizer around the drip line, where the feeder roots will be in highest concentration, and water it in. You can consult the nursery staff where you bought your tree for advice on its specific needs.

• *Pruning*. Damaged or dead wood can be cut off any time of year. However, if you're pruning for shape, try to do it while the tree is dormant, usually in early spring before its buds open. If you have fruit trees, consider removing all or most of the fruit for the first two years. Your tree will divert the energy it saves into growing and getting established.

• *Pests*. Rodents, cats, and dogs can be kept away from tender bark with a commercial wrap, or with several layers of burlap. Deer, however, require a fence. For insect or disease problems, contact your nursery for advice, or call a professional arborist.

WHAT'S NEXT

When you plant a tree with your kids, it makes them curious about *all* trees. A fun way to learn more about them is to learn to identify them. Knowing a tree by its shape and bark and leaves makes it a familiar and welcoming part of your world. Suddenly, a walk through the forest becomes a visit with old friends.

There are many field guides to native trees. Choose one that covers your particular region and shows overall shape, bark, foliage, and seasonal change.

SAFETY TIPS

For most of the chapters in this book, the safety tips are aimed at the kids. But when it comes to planting trees, the person at greatest risk is the one with the middle-aged back.

Dirt, whether it's wrapped around a root ball or on the end of a shovel, is very heavy. If you have to move it around, be smart. Get some help when you transport a heavy tree. When you lift, get as close as you can to the load, bend your knees, and keep your back straight. When you're digging, don't fill the shovel with the biggest clod of dirt you can balance on the blade. Take a little at a time. It isn't a race.

TREES AND TRADITIONS

Human beings have included trees in their traditions and rituals since the beginning of recorded time.

• In many parts of Asia, ancient trees are thought to house both spirits and gods. For the holiest ones, offerings are laid at their roots as they might be at an altar.

• Northwest Native Americans revered the giant red cedar as the central icon of their culture. It provided lumber for their houses, huge logs for their canoes and totem poles, and even fabric for their ceremonial clothes.

• In Jewish tradition, a tree is often planted at the birth of a child, sometimes using the afterbirth to fertilize the soil. When the child grows up and marries, the branches of their tree are used to build the canopy under which they are wed.

You and your child can plan your own ritual when you plant your tree. You could mark a birth, or a death, or some other transition or change. Kids have an inherent love of ritual. It adds meaning to life— and meaning is something we all crave.

WHAT DO TREES EAT AND BREATHE?

Let's say you had a pot full of soil that weighed exactly a hundred pounds. Then you planted a seed in that soil and it grew into a forty-pound tree. If you removed the tree with all of its roots and weighed the pot of soil again, how much would it weigh? The answer is, very close to a hundred pounds. So where did the forty pounds of tree come from? Photosynthesis.

Photosynthesis means "make with light." That's exactly what the tree does. It uses the energy in sunlight to combine carbon dioxide from the air with water from the ground. The soil provides minerals that the tree needs, but only in very small amounts. A tree puts all those things together to make its own wood and the food it needs to grow. In the process, it gives off oxygen, which is what humans and all other animals need to breathe.

Through photosynthesis, trees maintain the balance in our environment. They turn sunlight into fuel and food, they use up the carbon dioxide produced by our factories and engines, and they produce oxygen for all of us to breathe.

LEAFY GIANTS

Great trees have a way of capturing our imagination. Some are so impressive that we've given them their own names. Here are a few examples:

• The tallest living tree is a 367-foot redwood named Mendocino Tree, near Ukiah, California.

• The oldest living tree is a bristlecomb pine in the Nevada desert named Methuselah. It first sprouted up from the ground 4,765 years ago.

• The biggest tree by sheer mass is a giant sequoia named the General Sherman Tree, in California's Sequoia National Park. It would tip the scales at about 2,200 tons. But the largest organism on earth is a 200-acre grove of quaking aspens in Utah with a common root system and identical DNA. It's affectionately known as *Pando*, which is Latin for "I spread," and it weighs in at about 6,600 tons.

STUPID TREE JOKES

Q: What kind of tree will pinch you if you get too close?
A: A crab apple.

Q: What tree should you never pick a fight with?
A: Spruce Lee.

Q: How do you get an elephant down from a tall tree?
A: Put him on a leaf and wait until autumn.

Q: What kind of tree fits inside your hand?
A: A palm tree.

5
RIDE A BIKE

"People told me having a baby is like riding a bike—once you've done it you never forget how. They just didn't tell me the first ride is the Tour de France."

—One of my patients, a day after giving birth to an eight pound seven ounce boy

When I was a kid, we rode "chopper bikes." They were low-slung beauties with big banana seats and handlebars that swept back like the horns of mythical beasts. We used to collect scrap lumber from around the neighborhood so we could build jumping ramps at the bottom of steep hills. We'd pause at the top to rev our handlebars like Evel Knievel, then launch ourselves down the slope at a breakneck speed. No helmets. No pads. No guts, no glory.

Sometimes I wonder how any of us survived to adulthood.

My first lessons in bike riding took a similiar kamikaze approach. I don't think my father meant them to be that way—he just didn't know any better. He did it the same way countless parents have done it for years. He ran along with me for a few yards, holding the bike up to build my confidence. Then he let go. After ripping open my jeans and bloodying both of my knees, I finally stayed up. A few days later I was riding around the neighborhood looking for a ramp.

When it came time to teach my daughter how to ride, I set aside my overprotective parental instincts and trotted out the same time-honored approach. Big mistake. My daughter's approach to life is what you might call "risk aversive." When I told her that I planned to run along with her for a while and then let go, she slammed on the brakes and jumped off. I ended up pushing the bike home. But to tell you the truth, I was kind of relieved.

Luckily, a friend of mine told me about a method that better suits the parental paranoia of our times. My daughter learned to ride her bike in one day, and now she cruises all over the neighborhood looking for trouble. I just make sure she wears a helmet, and I hide all of our lumber before she gets any ideas.

WHEN TO START

Riding a bike safely requires balance and coordination, and at least a little bit of judgment. Most kids get there between the ages of five and seven, but as always, there are exceptions, both younger and older.

WHAT YOU NEED BEFORE YOU START

A Bicycle

Bikes come in all shapes and styles, and for the purpose of learning, most will do. The crucial issue is size. Most children start out on bikes with either sixteen- or twenty-inch wheels. Your kid should be able to straddle the horizontal bar at the top of the frame with one leg on each side and both feet flat on the ground. In this position, there should be about two inches of clearance between the child's crotch and the top of the bar. If you use a girl's frame with no horizontal bar (and no real practical advantage, as far as I know), you'll have to estimate where that bar would be.

Adjust the seat so your child's leg is nearly (but not quite) straight when the pedal reaches its lowest point. Make sure she isn't sliding off to one side to reach the pedal. The handlebars probably won't need too much adjustment, as long as your kid is fairly upright and comfortable while grabbing them.

Fancy bikes with multiple gears aren't necessary, and sometimes they're confusing. A cheap, one-gear kid's bike should be fine, so long as it's the right size. Pedal brakes are slower than hand brakes, but they make it easier for small kids to exert enough force to stop a speeding bike. Either is okay so long as you test them out right at the start. On a bike with hand brakes, make sure there are two, and teach your child to use both at once.

Protective Gear

Helmets are absolutely mandatory. Make sure the helmet fits snugly in place without causing discomfort. It should rock only a little from front to back, and almost not at all from side to side. Adjust the strap so that one finger just fits between the strap and the chin. If you already have knee pads, elbow pads, and gloves—for in-line skating, for instance—they aren't a bad idea. Anything that reduces the fear of falling can help. Long sleeves, long pants, and sneakers are also a good idea. Make sure there aren't any loose shoelaces or pieces of clothing to get caught in the gears.

As long as we're talking about clothing, we should mention what *you'll* be wearing. You're in for a lot of running, so dress appropriately.

A Place to Practice

The requirements here are pretty simple. You'll need a surface that's big, flat, open, hard, and smooth. Empty parking lots and paved playgrounds are the best. In a pinch, basketball or tennis courts can work, but they're a little tight, and they tend to have those inconvenient metal poles.

Snacks

This is going to be a lot of fun, but it'll also be hard, physical work for both of you. Bring something to eat and drink, and remember to stop once in a while to rest.

BASIC TECHNIQUE

Training Wheels

The problem with training wheels is that they do exactly what they're supposed to. They keep the bike from tipping over. Essentially, they turn a bicycle into a tricycle, and they keep a child from learning to stay upright on her own. Nevertheless, they have their place. With training wheels, your child can learn to pedal, steer, and stop the bike without worrying about life and limb. Let her master those skills first. After that, the training wheels come off. If you've bought a new bike for your child to learn on, let her get used to it with training wheels first. Learning to ride is hard enough without adjusting to a brand-new bike.

The Tablecloth Method

This approach has some definite advantages. It provides a lot of safety and security, so it's especially good if either one of you is fearful about the possibility of a fall. The downside is that it requires a lot of work on your part.

First, find a tablecloth or similar piece of fabric that can serve as a harness. It should be long enough to wrap around your kid's chest and under her arms, with enough left over to gather up behind her and grasp easily in one hand.

Position the bike at one end of your practice area, with a lot of room in front of you. Put the tablecloth around your kid and grasp it firmly behind her. Hold the cloth very close to her body—you want to start out with maximum control when she starts to tilt or swerve. Steady the bike by holding the handlebar as she climbs aboard.

Start moving forward slowly, keeping upward tension on the tablecloth. As soon as you get going, let go of the handlebar. Now you're holding her up just with the pressure you apply on the harness. Keep that pressure nice and firm—you want her to feel as if she couldn't fall over even if she tried.

Jog along beside her, keeping the pressure steady. Tell her to focus on a point in the distance and go in a straight line. If she starts to swerve or tilt even a little, use the tablecloth to get her back on track. When you get near the end of the practice area, tell her to apply the brakes gently so she doesn't jam them on and fly over the handlebars. When she comes to a full stop, help her slide forward off the seat and step to one side. The first dismount may be a bit rough, so talk her through it.

Now, turn around and head back the other way. This time have her pedal a little faster. The faster she goes, the more stable she should be. When she seems to be reaching a balance point, ease up a little on the tablecloth. As soon as she begins to tilt or swerve, pull her back upright. Don't let her tip too far, or you won't be able to bring her back. With each new run, ease up a little more. Gradually, her own sense of balance will take over, and she will require less and less pressure on the harness, for shorter and shorter amounts of time. Don't forget to practice the full stop and dismount at the end of each run.

Eventually you'll come to a point where she can do an entire run without you applying any real pressure on the harness. When she's done this several times and she has mastered the dismount, let her try a short run on her own. Grasp the back of the seat to steady her at the start, and let go as soon as she has some momentum. Tell her to stop before she takes on too much speed. Make each subsequent run a little longer.

Once she reaches this point, she's home free. When she can do a long, straight run with confidence, add a gentle curve. It's a good idea to slow down a little going into the turn, and then pedal again coming out of it. Next come big circles, first in one direction, then the other. Gradually, make the circles a little tighter. After that you can try figure eights, slaloms, and anything else you can think of.

The "Low Rider" Method

This is an alternative approach if you don't have the foot speed or the strength to use the tablecloth method. It works especially well with independent kids who like to do things for themselves, or for very frightened kids who need to feel that they're in control at all times.

As before, it's a good idea to have your kids use the training wheels first, so they're comfortable with the mechanics of pedaling, stopping, and steering.

Lower the seat on the bicycle as far as it will go and tighten it in place. Your child should be able to stand with both feet on the ground while sitting in the seat. If the seat is still too high, you might have to borrow a slightly smaller bike. Next, remove the pedals from the bike. Note that the two pedals unscrew in opposite directions. If you have trouble removing the pedals, you can still use this method by positioning them horizontally so they don't interfere with your child's feet, but it can be a hassle keeping them that way.

On a nice, flat practice area, have your kid sit on the shortened seat and propel herself by walking with her feet on either side. As she gains confidence, she'll start to run. Encourage her to glide a little by picking up her feet slightly (just an inch or two will do). As her balance improves, her glide time will get longer. Finally, have her push off on both sides at once and glide with her feet resting on the base of the pedals. During the glide, she can experiment with turning and steering.

Now that she can balance and turn, the rest is easy. Readjust the seat to the proper height and put the pedals back on. Proceed as you would for the tablecloth method after the tablecloth has been removed.

The Downhill Method

This approach works great in combination with the low-rider method, and it works with the tablecloth method, too. The idea is to separate the three main tasks of bike riding—balance, steering, and propulsion—and let your child learn them one at a time.

Find a stretch of pavement that goes down a gentle hill, then flattens out for a considerable distance. A sloping parking lot is best, but a road on a hill with no traffic will do the trick. You can even use a grassy hill if you want to slow things down and cushion any falls, but choose one that's closely mown and as smooth as possible. Bumps can be distracting, and high grass doesn't allow the bike to gain momentum.

Have your kid get on the bike far enough up the hill so that once she gets started, she can roll down the slope at a modest speed. From here, proceed as before with your chosen method, but for the initial steps have your kid glide down the hill without pedaling. Once she can glide in a straight line and brake to a stop, add some gentle turns.

By this point your kid will have learned the two most difficult tasks in riding a bike: keeping balanced and steering. Now all she has to do is propel the bike without messing up what she's already learned. At first, have her glide down the hill and pedal a short distance at the end of the run as the slope flattens out. With each subsequent run, she'll gain confidence and pedal a little farther. Eventually, there'll be a run where she comes down the hill, starts to pedal, and just keeps going.

Starting

Overcoming inertia requires a leap of faith. When the bike isn't moving, it isn't stable, and kids can sense this. The hardest thing about starting is not being tentative. You need to push off hard enough to get up some momentum.

Position the pedals so the higher one is a little more forward than straight up (somewhere around the "two o'clock" position if you're viewing the right-foot pedal from the right side of the bike). Your kid should plant her feet firmly on either side of the bike, with one foot *behind* the low pedal. Both hands should be on the handlebars.

The next step involves three movements that have to take place simultaneously. Your child must step onto the higher pedal, push off with the other foot, and hold the handlebars steady. Failure to do any of these things will result in a fall.

Use the tablecloth around your child's chest or a hand on the back of the seat to steady her. Encourage her to push off hard to get some forward momentum as soon as possible, and give her a little push at first if she needs it. Most important, be patient. It's a complicated task and may take some practice.

TROUBLESHOOTING

Big Swerves

The problem with steering a bicycle is that it's counterintuitive. As we start to tilt to one side, our first impulse is to turn the handlebars away from the fast-approaching pavement. Unfortunately, this just makes the problem worse. In order to right ourselves, we have to turn *into* the fall.

Most kids will figure this out by trial and error as they try to stay upright on a moving bike. But a few will keep following instinct and turn away from the fall, resulting in big swerves as they try desperately to keep themselves upright. For those kids, try asking them to consciously turn toward the side they're falling to. Sometimes a little light-bulb goes off and they suddenly straighten things out.

"Don't Let Go!"

There are some kids who seem ready to take off on their own, but they panic every time you let go. Here, the key is patience. Avoid the temptation to promise you'll hold on, and then let go. Sure, it might work. But it's just as likely they'll panic and fall, then stare up at you with that wounded look that says: "How could you betray me?"

Sooner or later they'll get enough confidence to allow you to let go. You might bargain with them, saying you'll let go just at the end of the run and they can stop the bike ten feet later. Soon, ten feet becomes twenty, then thirty, and the problem is past. But don't try to trick them. Let them stay in their comfort zone.

Getting Past a Crash

Even with the methods outlined above, falls can happen. When they do, pay attention to your kid's reaction. If she gets up and jumps back on the bike, don't give her confusing messages by going into an overprotective panic. On the other hand, if she seems shaken and scared, don't force her to try again. Get out the water and snacks. Tell her how proud you are, and review how much progress she's made. Let the sting go away. Then, if she wants to give it another try, go for it. If not, pack it in for the day. There's always tomorrow.

SAFETY TIPS

The Importance of Helmets

A group of researchers in Seattle did a study involving victims of bicycle accidents. They found that the people who were not wearing helmets were at significant risk of serious head injury and long-term neurological deficits. And what about the people who *were* wearing helmets? How many do you think had long-term brain damage? Zero. None. Nada.

Bike helmets are cheap. Brains aren't. Even a kid riding around in the driveway can fall and smack his head on the curb. If your kid rides a bike, he should wear a helmet. By the way, the same goes for you. Be a good example. Your brain is worth something too.

Rules of the Road

When young kids start riding bikes, you should tell them to act as pedestrians. They should stick to the sidewalk and walk the bike across streets. Once they're old enough to ride in the street, make sure they understand traffic. Have them stick to the right side of the road and stop at intersections. Teach them proper turn signals. Most of all, observe them while they're riding to make sure their actions match your words.

Equipment

Make sure your kids have reflectors on the front and back of their bikes, and some kind of horn or bell. And if they ride near dusk or after dark, they need bright, reflective clothing and a light. Discourage sandals and slip-on or open-toed shoes while riding, and watch out for loose clothing or shoelaces that can tangle up in gears.

TWO-WHEELED WONDERS

• The first known bicycle was made entirely of wood. It was built in 1791 and displayed in Paris, France, as a two-wheeled "wooden horse."

• The longest and most grueling bicycle race is the yearly Race Across America. Riders cover three thousand miles in about ten days.

• The fastest "bicycle" ever timed was an enclosed, aerodynamic bike pedaled by Sam Whittingham in October 2001. After a flying start, he maintained a speed of 80.55 mph over a flat, 200-meter course.

BICYCLE SCIENCE

Did you ever wonder why you can balance on a bicycle while it's moving, but as soon as it stops you tip over? The reason is something called angular momentum.

Regular momentum is the tendency of objects to stay at the same speed. Things that are moving want to keep moving, and things that are still want to stay still. But when an object is spinning, it has *angular* momentum. Not only does it want to keep spinning, it wants to keep spinning in the same plane.

Try this. Remove the front wheel from one of your bicycles and hold it on either side by its axle. Have someone else slap the wheel to get it spinning as fast as it will go. Now try to tilt the wheel out of its plane. You'll feel a lot of resistance, as if someone grabbed the wheel and tried to twist it. Let your children try it too. The wheel wants to stay in one plane. When you ride a bike, both wheels want to stay upright.

Now, have your kids stand up on a chair that swivels. Spot them so they don't fall. Give them the wheel and try the trick again. This time, when they tilt the top of the wheel to the left, the chair will swivel to the left. When they tilt it to the right, the chair turns right. This is why you can steer a bicycle without actually turning the handlebars. All you have to do is lean.

A spinning object like a bicycle wheel is called a gyroscope. Gyroscopes do much more than keep bikes from falling over. They keep satellites stable in space and help airline pilots know how much they're tilting their wings.

A BICYCLE BRAINTEASER

Imagine a bike with no one on it, balanced upright on its two wheels, with one pedal straight up and the other straight down. What happens when you push the bottom pedal backward? Which way does the bike go? Which way do the pedals turn? Think you know? Okay, now go try it.

STUPID BICYCLE JOKES

Q: Why can't an elephant ride a bike?
A: It doesn't have a thumb to ring the bell.

Q: Why can't a flower ride a bike?
A: It might lose its *petals*.

Q: Why can't bicycles stand up on their own?
A: Because they're *two tired*.

6
BAKE BREAD

> "Then do not grasp at the stars, but do life's plain,
> common work as it comes, certain that daily duties and
> daily bread are the sweetest things in life."
>
> —Robert Louis Stevenson

I joined a hippie, co-op dormitory in college because I thought the rooms were nice. I wasn't prepared when, on my first day there, they told me I had to sign up for a house job. Cook crew was all filled, and I didn't want to clean toilets or wash dishes. That left bread duty.

When I walked into the kitchen, I was amazed at how big everything was. Meals for fifty came out of there every day, so all the appliances and equipment were twice the normal size. I felt like Jack in the Giant's castle.

A woman in tank top and overalls was standing at the huge butcher-block table, pouring flour into a measuring cup the size of a bucket. Her curly brown hair stuck out in puffs from the sides of her red bandanna. "Hi," she said. "I'm Gigi."

I told her I'd never made bread before and that I should probably just watch for a while.

She laughed. "You can't learn to make bread by watching! You have to dive in. Here, put about five cups of warm water in here."

She handed me the biggest mixing bowl I'd ever seen. In the bottom was a coarse brown powder that smelled like beer. I walked over to the tap and turned on the hot water. Before I could put the bowl under the faucet, Gigi snatched it out of my hands.

"Warm," she said. "If it's too hot, you'll kill it."

"Kill what?"

"The yeast. Bread is alive."

Okay, now I was worried. This whole cooperative-living thing was going to be hard enough as it was. I wasn't ready for live bread.

We pushed and kneaded the dough as if they were giant balls of Silly Putty, then set them aside under damp cotton towels. An hour later, by the sorcery of the Giant's kitchen, they had doubled in size. We divided them into blackened loaf pans to rise again, then slid them into the hot ovens.

As the scent of the baking bread drifted through the dorm, people started coming down from their rooms. Someone took out a chunk of butter the size of a brick and a one-gallon can of honey. By the time the first loaves came out, there was a crowd around the breadboard.

"This is his first bread," said Gigi. "Let him have the honors."

I cut into a loaf, and steam rose into the air. I took a crusty piece off the end and slathered it with butter, then drizzled honey on top until it ran down my hand. I took a bite. It was so good I moaned.

That night, I stayed up late and hung out talking at the breadboard. I made a bunch of new friends, and started thinking about politics for the first time in my life. By the time I went to sleep, I was wondering what I'd look like in a bandanna.

Never underestimate the power of freshly baked bread.

WHEN TO START

Working with dough is no more complicated than working with Silly Putty, and it's just as much fun for kids of all ages. However, if your kids are young, take special precautions around open ovens and hot bread pans.

WHAT YOU NEED BEFORE YOU START

Equipment

Large mixing bowl (plastic or stainless steel is light and unbreakable)
Measuring cup
Measuring spoons
Bread pans (one 9 by 5 inches, or two 8 by 4 inches)
Sturdy mixing spoon
Large bread board (wood, glass, plastic, or stone)

> Plain aluminum pans work fine. If you wipe them out with a dry paper towel after each use, you don't even have to wash them. Over time they build up a nice, black patina that's virtually nonstick. Glass also works, but it's slippery and breakable, and it may throw off the cooking time.

Ingredients (for a Basic White Bread)

1 tablespoon sugar
¼ cup warm water (bath temperature, around 100 to 105° F)
1 package (¼ ounce) active dry yeast
1 cup milk
3½ tablespoons butter
1 tablespoon salt
About 4 cups unbleached, all-purpose flour (you may not use all of this)

1 tablespoon vegetable oil
(optional: 1 egg white; 1 teaspoon sesame or poppy seeds)

BASIC TECHNIQUE

The entire process is well within the ability of most kids. You may need to help them with measurements and timing, but mostly you get to sit back and watch.

Step 1: Start the yeast

Dissolve the sugar in the warm water, and check to make sure it's about the temperature of a warm bath. Add the yeast, and stir until it's well dissolved. In a few minutes bubbles should begin to form and the top of the mixture should start to look foamy.

If you pulled an old yeast packet from the back of your cupboard, this is when you find out if it's still alive. If you don't get any bubbles, buy some fresh yeast.

Step 2: Mix the dough

Heat up the milk and 3 tablespoons of the butter in the microwave or on the stove. The butter should be melted, and the mixture should be about bath temperature again. Add the yeast mixture, and then mix in the salt and about 2 cups of the flour. Scrape the bottom of the bowl, and add more flour a little at a time until the dough becomes too stiff to mix with a spoon.

Step 3: Kneading

Put the breadboard on a sturdy table or counter, with a damp towel in between to keep it from sliding around. You may want to get a small footstool so your child can work at about waist level. Spread a little flour on the board and on your child's hands, then turn the dough out onto the center of the board.

Flatten the dough into an elongated circle with the heel of the hand, then fold it in half. Turn the dough 90 degrees, then flatten and fold again. Repeat this motion for about five or ten minutes, reflouring both board and hands whenever the dough sticks to them. I can't tell you precisely how much flour you'll need. Just add a little whenever the dough gets sticky.

As kneading continues, the dough will become more rubbery and resistant. When you can press your thumb in about a half-inch and the dough springs back all the way, it's done.

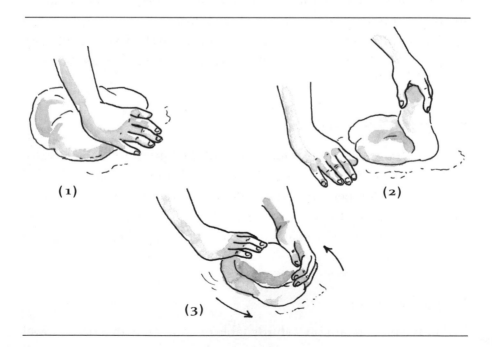

(1)

(2)

(3)

Step 4: First rising

Clean out the mixing bowl and dry it thoroughly. Put a little vegetable oil in the bottom and roll the dough around in it until all sides are coated. Cover the bowl with a clean, damp towel and leave it in a warm place where it won't be disturbed. Go do something fun and come back in about an hour.

Step 5: Forming the loaves

When you take off the towel, something magical will have occurred. The dough will have doubled in size. Let your child punch down the dough with his fists (definitely a highlight of the bread-making process) and roll it out onto the floured breadboard. If you have two smaller pans, divide the dough in half. Knead it lightly a few times just to give it some shape, then pull it together into a loaf shape that will fit in the pans.

Take the remaining butter and grease the inside of the pans thoroughly, especially in the corners where the bread is more likely to stick. Place the loaves in the pans, making sure any seams are on the bottom. Cover the bread and let it rise until it doubles in size again, this time about forty-five minutes.

Step 6: Final touches

Once the loaves have risen, preheat the oven to 375°F, with a rack on the next to lowest level. If you want to give the loaf a handsome sheen, mix 1 egg white with a couple of teaspoons of water and brush it lightly across the tops of the loaves. A sprinkle of sesame or poppy seeds at this point adds a nice touch.

Just before putting the bread in the oven, use a sharp, serrated knife to slice three, shallow, diagonal cuts in the "skin" at the top of the dough. Make them about a quarter-inch deep. This allows the steam to escape and keeps the top of the loaf from cracking.

Put the loaf in the center of the oven. If you have two loaves, separate them by a couple of inches. Set the timer for twenty-five minutes, or thirty if it's one large loaf.

Step 7: Fresh bread!

Timing bread is an imprecise art. It depends on the size and composition of the pans, the accuracy of the oven thermostat, the amount of dough, and even the altitude. Like deciding how much flour the dough needed, it has to be done by feel.

Start checking the loaves at about twenty-five minutes. Once they look golden brown, turn them gently out of their pans onto a cooling rack. Thump the bottom of the loaves with your finger. If the bottom is firm and brown and sounds hollow when you thump it, it's done. If you aren't sure, you can use an instant meat thermometer inserted into the center of the loaf from the bottom. It should read at least 200°F when done.

Leave the loaf on the rack on its side to let the steam escape. Let it cool and firm up for a while before you cut it—about twenty minutes, or as long as your willpower permits. If there's any left over, store it in a paper bag or just leave it cutside down on the breadboard. Don't store it in plastic, or the crust will get soft.

It should stay fresh for about a day, and after that it makes great French toast.

TROUBLESHOOTING

The Dough Falls Apart When You Knead It

This is usually the result of too much flour on the surface of the dough. Clear excess flour from the board and keep kneading it. Unless you've added way too much flour already, the dough should start holding together again.

The Dough Won't Rise

There are several possible reasons for this. If the room is very cold, the dough will rise slowly. Try putting it in a slightly warm oven. Also, make sure that you aren't using ancient, dead yeast, and that you didn't kill your yeast by dissolving it in water that was too hot.

The Dough Rose Too Much

If you forget your dough and let it rise too long, the yeast may become overly enthusiastic. The dough will smell strongly of alcohol and become spongy. Never fear—it can still be saved. Mix the dough with another cup of milk. Mix two more cups of flour with more sugar and salt, and knead it into the moistened dough. Let it rise again, and proceed as you would have, this time with a double batch.

Wrong Pan Size

Remember that your loaves will continue to grow even as they bake. If they're already full before you put them in the oven, your pans are too small. If the unbaked dough fills a pan more than three-fourths full, divide the dough in half and bake it as two loaves instead.

Cracked Top

This is usually a sign of too much flour, leaving the loaf with insufficient "give" as it bakes and rises. On the other hand, a free-form loaf like a braid that spreads out too much has too little flour.

Top Too Brown

When the top of the loaf turns brown long before the loaf is done, put a little aluminum foil loosely over it. This will keep it from over-browning. You can also lower the oven temperature by 25 degrees and leave it in a little longer.

Big Holes

Some rustic breads are supposed to have larger, uneven holes. But for the basic recipe provided, large holes mean insufficient kneading or overrising.

WHAT'S NEXT

Once this basic recipe is mastered, there's no end to the kinds of bread you can make. For a healthier loaf, substitute whole-wheat flour for up to a third of the white flour. Try cinnamon rolls, or bagels. Put in nuts, or raisins, or herbs. Experiment. Have fun.

You can also try baking different shapes. After the first rising, roll the dough into three long strands and tie them into a loose braid. Let it rise again, then bake it on a greased cookie sheet. Or sculpt the dough into a teddy bear and add some doughy facial features just before putting it in the oven.

SAFETY TIPS

It's never too early to start talking to your kids about kitchen hazards. The majority of burns and house fires take place in the kitchen, and it's probably the most dangerous room in the house, as far as your kids are concerned.

Here are some good rules to follow:

1. Only adults may turn on the stove and oven, or open the oven door.
2. When a hot oven is opened, everyone in the kitchen should be warned, and no small children should be within ten feet of it unless held by an adult.
3. Nothing is placed in or removed from a hot oven without full-sized oven mitts.
4. There is a working fire extinguisher within easy reach of the kitchen at all times.
5. There is a working smoke alarm in the kitchen or an adjoining room.

IT'S ALIVE!

My friend Gigi was right, bread is a living thing. Or actually, billions of living things.

In ancient Egypt about six thousand years ago, people first realized that if they left dough out for a while before baking it, it would rise. Bread made from risen dough was lighter and tastier than flat, unleavened bread. But what was causing the transformation?

The answer is yeast. Yeast are single-celled fungi. Their spores float around in the air until they find a source of moisture and food that will let them grow and reproduce. The Egyptians captured naturally occurring yeast by leaving their bread dough out in the open air. We use dried, compressed yeast that has been grown and processed especially for baking. One gram of baker's yeast contains about seven billion yeast cells.

Once yeast is exposed to moisture and food (in the form of starch or sugar), it begins to grow and multiply. It uses enzymes to break down starch into sugar, and then convert sugar into alcohol, carbon dioxide gas, and energy. This is called fermentation, and it's the same process that produces alcohol in wine, beer, and liquor. That's why bread dough smells a little like beer as it rises or bakes.

The carbon dioxide forms little gas pockets in the dough, making it rise. As the bread bakes, the gas expands, and the bread rises even more.

"WHY ARE WE GIVING THE BREAD A MASSAGE?"

That's what my daughter asked the first time we made bread together. It's a good question. As you knead the dough, it becomes more elastic. This allows it to retain the tiny bubbles of carbon dioxide made by the yeast, and to stretch as those bubbles expand. But why does "massaging" the dough make this happen? The key is something called gluten.

Different parts of the wheat kernel contain different proteins. When the wheat is ground into flour, these proteins are mixed together, and when water is added to the flour, the proteins combine in new ways.

When we knead a lump of dough, the wheat proteins called glutenin and gliadin are stretched out and pushed together. This allows them to form chemical bonds called cross-links. When they combine in this way, they form a new substance called gluten.

Cross-link bonds are also found in rubber and chewing gum. They allow molecules to move in relationship to each other without coming apart. The result is elasticity.

Different kinds of flour have different amounts of gluten. Bread flour has a lot, in order to make the dough stretchy. Cake flour has much less, which keeps the cake tender. Nonwheat flours, like rye or oat, have only a little gluten, and usually need to be combined with wheat flour to make bread.

THE BEGGAR, THE BAKER, AND THE KING

Once there was a poor beggar woman who could barely scrape together enough money to keep herself alive. Each day, she would satisfy her hunger by lingering outside the bakery and inhaling the smell of fresh-baked bread. This, she said, was her morning feast, and she used it to sustain her through the better part of each day.

One day, the baker spied her outside his shop and rushed outside to confront her.

"You there! Old woman! What are you doing?"

"I am stopping to enjoy the smell of your bread," she replied.

"I worked hard to make that bread," he said. "Since you have enjoyed it so, you will pay me for my work."

The baker seized the old woman by the arm and dragged her to the local authorities. No one there had ever heard of such a case, and they couldn't decide what to do. Finally, they appealed to King Solomon and asked him to resolve the situation.

"Yes," said the wise king, "the baker has a point. It is his bread that she smells, and therefore he must be paid. Old woman, do you have any money?"

The old woman held out her hand. In it were two small coins. "They are all I have in the world," she said.

Solomon took the coins and clinked them together in his palm, then gave them back to the old woman.

"What is this?" demanded the baker. "Am I not to be paid?"

"Of course," said Solomon. "She has just paid you for the smell of your bread—with the sound of her coins."

7
FLY A KITE

"O human race born to fly upward, wherefore at a little wind dost thou fall."

—*Dante Alighieri*

When I was growing up, there was a kite-eating tree in our yard. It wasn't like a leopard that leaps out of hiding to attack its prey. It was more like a giant Venus flytrap.

Our kites were drawn to it by some mysterious, wind-born scent, or maybe an invisible magnetic field. We tried to drag them back to safety, but sooner or later they would always wrap themselves around it and expire in a twisting dance of death. For months afterward we would watch the wind and rain digest each kite a little at a time. Soon there'd be nothing left but a skeleton of sun-bleached sticks and string.

My favorite kite was a Batman kite we got on sale at Kmart. It was jet-black, except for the yellow bat insignia, and as sleek and powerful as its namesake when it soared and darted in the wind. We kept it away from the tree for almost a year—wetting our fingers to test the breeze before each takeoff and aborting any flight at the first sign of danger. But alas, on a stormy day of wicked, shifting winds, even the bat kite succumbed to the tree's siren call.

After that we changed our strategy. We started making homemade kites out of cheap materials, and we flew them with impunity in any kind of weather. The loss of kites was staggering, but we no longer mourned. The tree demanded sacrifice. If we wanted to fly in his domain, we had to pay the price.

WHEN TO START

Making and flying kites is a great activity for kids of all ages. The materials are cheap and easy to work with, so everyone can make and decorate their own. In a light wind, even kids as young as three or four can help fly a kite once it's up.

WHAT YOU NEED BEFORE YOU START

Whenever you build a kite, there's a trade-off between weight and durability. If you live someplace where there are often heavy winds to contend with, you'll want to use stronger materials. If you're expecting only a modest breeze, build the lightest kite you can put together.

Tools

Scissors, or a utility knife
A hole punch
A yardstick (or a measuring tape and a separate straight edge)

Materials (for One Kite)

• *One 40 by 36-inch sheet of cardboard or paper to make a pattern.* For onetime use, any paper will do, and you can tape smaller sheets together if you wish. Use cardboard if you plan to keep the pattern and make more than one kite.

• *One 40 by 36-inch sheet of plastic*. All-purpose plastic from any hardware store works great, and often comes in white or clear, which are both easy to decorate. A thickness of 2.0 mil is light, but fairly tough. Heavy duty, extra large garbage bags will work, but many are only 1.0 mil, so they may not hold up to a stiff wind or a crash landing. Use 1.0 mil plastic for light winds, when low weight is essential. For very heavy winds, get 3.0 or 4.0 mil.

• *Two 36-inch hardwood dowels*. These are easy to find at the hardware store. A diameter of one-quarter inch is standard, but one-eighth inch is much lighter and will help get the kite aloft in light winds. If you can find them, thin bamboo sticks that are sold in garden stores are very light and very strong, but make sure you use ones that are straight.

• *Duct tape or strong cloth tape*.

• *Clear packing tape*.

• *One 12-foot length of string, to serve as a bridle*. Kite string will do, but something a little stronger will last longer.

• *Stickers and permanent marking pens, or latex or acrylic paint, for decoration*.

MAKING THE KITE

The kite we're going to make is a classic design known as the "Scott Sled." It gets its name from two side flaps that look like the runners of a sled, and from its inventor, Frank Scott. Scott introduced it in 1964 as a variation on an earlier design by William Allison.

This is the first kite I ever made. It flies well even in light winds, and it's so stable that even young children can keep it aloft. The only exception is in very shifty winds, where a sudden gust from the side can collapse the kite and send it plummeting to earth.

Start by gathering together your tools and materials and studying the diagram. You and your child can work as a team. Remember not to take over the project—most kids can construct this kite with only a little bit of assistance. You may want to make two kites—one out of light dowels and plastic, and another for heavy-duty use. This is easy to do once you've made a cardboard pattern, and it allows you to adjust to different strengths of wind.

Step 1: Make a pattern

On your large sheet of paper or cardboard, draw a rectangle 36 inches high and 40 inches wide, using a yardstick or straight edge to keep things neat. Along the top and bottom edges, make four pencil marks 10 inches in from each corner. On the side edges make two more marks, 10 inches down from the top corners. Using your straight edge to connect these marks, draw the sides of the kite as shown in the drawing.

The triangle in the center of the kite will be cut out to create a vent. This stabilizes the kite, especially in strong winds. Draw the triangle as shown.

Carefully cut out the paper pattern, including the vent. You can fold it in half along the midline to make sure both sides are exactly the same. Trim off any stray edges until the kite is perfectly symmetric.

Step 2: Cut the sail

Place the paper on top of your plastic and trace around it with a marker, being very careful to keep the plastic perfectly flat and the pattern in one place until the tracing is done. Remove the pattern, saving it for later use, and cut out the kite. Try to leave only straight, smooth edges—stray cuts can develop into tears and tatter your kite in a stiff breeze. Use packing tape to reinforce the plastic by the corners of the vent, where tearing is also a danger.

Step 3: Attach the dowels

Lay your dowels on top of the kite, as shown, and secure them with packing tape. Four or five pieces on each dowel should be enough, but keep them symmetric. The string will attach to the corners on either side of the kite. Use a double layer of duct tape to reinforce them, then punch a hole in each corner, about an inch in from the edge.

Step 4: Attach the bridle

Tie one end of the 12-foot length of string through each hole. At the exact center of the string, double it and tie it in a knot, creating a fixed loop. This is where the kite string will attach.

Step 5: Final touches

When the kite is in the air, the side with the sticks will be facing you, so that's the side you should decorate. Let your kid go wild with markers and stickers, but be careful with the paint. Thick layers will add weight, and they may make the kite asymmetric. Big, bold swatches of color look best when the kite is in the air. On clear plastic, the paint and markers give a nice stained-glass effect.

This kite doesn't need a tail in order to fly, but a couple of bright plastic or Mylar streamers add a little style. You can tape one tail to the bottom of each dowel.

FLYING TIPS

When and Where

Before you fly, scout around for an appropriate site: an open area without tall poles, overhead lines, busy streets, or kite-eating trees.

Ideally, you want a day with moderately strong, steady winds. Even if the wind on the ground seems too light, it may be better up high—check out the tops of nearby trees to see if this is the case. Really high winds will shred your kite, and gusty winds will be difficult for first-time flyers. Beaches are often a good bet, even when there's no wind anywhere else, especially in the afternoon (see below to find out why). For this kite, all you need is ten to fifteen miles per hour of steady wind.

The String's the Thing

There are a lot of choices when it comes to kite string. You can buy string that's especially made for kites, usually prewound on a plastic spool with handles. You can also get a spool of regular cotton or synthetic string and put a piece of dowel or a stick through it. Get at least a hundred yards worth, and make sure it's strong enough so you can't snap it between your two hands.

One final option is a stout fishing pole and a heavy-duty reel. You can leave off the top half of the pole if you like. You'll need at least twenty-pound test monofilament line, and thirty or forty might be better. This setup looks a little strange, but it's worth its weight in gold when you have to pull in two hundred yards of string in a stiff wind.

We Have Lift-off

To launch the kite, let your kid hold the spool and let out line, while you back away from them holding the kite by the bottom of the two dowels. Make sure the vent is at the bottom of the kite. You should be facing directly into the wind, and your child should have some running room behind her, in case she needs to pull a little to get the kite aloft.

When you've run off about thirty or forty feet of string, have your child tighten her grip and gently pull. As she pulls on the string, you should feel the kite begin to lift. On the count of three, release the kite just as your child takes a few steps backward. If there's not much wind, she may have to backpedal at first, letting out line a little at a time as she goes.

As she lets out string, the kite will dip a little. She should let out a few feet at a time, then stop to let the kite climb back up before she lets out any more. If the wind is light and shifty, she may have to give a quick pull or back up once in a while to keep tension on the string. Loss of tension is always a problem, but especially so for a Scott Sled, which will lose its shape and collapse if it isn't inflated.

Soft Landings

When it's time to bring the kite in for a landing, don't try to wind it all the way in or you'll end up crashing it into the ground, or on some unsuspecting bystander. Make sure the kite is coming in over an open area where it can land safely. Wind up the string until the kite starts to become unstable. As it nears the ground, walk toward it to take the tension off the string and let it flutter down gently, then wind up the remainder of the string.

TROUBLESHOOTING

Lopsided Kite

Sometimes a kite will veer or dip consistently to one side. This can be caused by an unbalanced or asymmetric kite, or by an asymmetric bridle. Try adjusting the knot on the bridle string to one side or the other. If the knot is too tight to undo, shorten the bridle on one side where it attaches to the kite.

Twisted Line

Sometimes, kite strings get twisted. If this is a persistent problem, you can attach the string to the bridle using a heavy fishing swivel. That should remove the twist and keep it from re-forming.

WHAT'S NEXT

Although stable kites, like the Scott Sled, are great for beginners, they aren't all that exciting once they're up in the air. If stable kites start to lose their allure, it's time to move on to *un*stable kites.

Stunt kites have two sets of double lines that attach to either wing. With surprisingly subtle movements, the operator can make them dip and dart through the air like crazed hummingbirds. They can be a little pricey, but they're tremendous fun.

SAFETY TIPS

Generally, kites are safe fun, but there are a few precautions to keep in mind.

When there are little kids around, loose string always seems to get wrapped around little fingers, wrists, ankles, and even necks. A big kite in a stiff wind can pull a string tight with surprising force, and the result is very unpleasant. The solution is proper string management. If the string isn't in the air, it should be on the spool.

Warm days and big wind sometimes mean a thunderstorm is on its way. The last thing you need is to be racing around an open area trying to wind up a hundred yards of string while Zeus takes target practice with his thunderbolts. At the first whisper of thunder, pack it in.

My only other warning has to do with an unlikely but costly possibility. Mylar is a very good conductor, and a Mylar kite tail that crosses power lines could knock out a nice little piece of a power grid. Don't laugh—I know someone who did it.

KITES AROUND THE WORLD

Kites were the first flying objects made by human beings. They were developed in China more than two thousand years ago, not only for amusement, but to send visual signals over long distances.

Eventually, kites appeared as far away as Egypt and Polynesia, probably developing there independently rather than spreading from the Far East.

In Japan, there is an ancient tradition of six-sided fighting kites called "Rokkaku." They are usually decorated with fierce, warrior images, and their strings are coated with tiny shards of glass to sever the lines of enemy kites.

LIFE'S A BEACH

Why is it always windy at the beach? To understand that, you need to know about temperature and density. When air on the earth's surface is warmed, it becomes less dense, and it rises. Cooler air then rushes in to take its place.

During the day, the sun heats up the land faster than the ocean, because water has a very high specific heat. That means it can absorb more energy with a smaller change in temperature. As the land heats up, it warms the air above it, which expands and rises. The cooler air above the ocean rushes in to take its place, and on the beach we feel it as wind.

This is why the wind at the beach gets stronger and stronger on those warm, summer afternoons, and why it always seems to blow inland from the sea.

KITING RECORDS

• The world's largest flying kite is the Mega-Ray of Elk Grove Park, California. It has 12,696 square feet of surface area, plus a 130-foot tail.

• The record for highest altitude for a single kite on a single string belongs to Richard P. Synergy. On Saturday, August 12, 2000, his meteorological kite reached a height of 14, 509 feet.

• On August 24, 2000, Ray Bethell of Long Beach, Washington, flew twenty-one kites simultaneously, in three stacks of seven kites each.

STUPID KITE JOKES

"Knock-knock."

"Who's there?"

"Augusta."

"Augusta who?"

"No one. It's just Augusta wind."

*   *   *

Say this one out loud, with a thick Aussie accent:

"Knock-knock."

"Who's there?"

"Kite."

"Kite who?"

"It's *Kite* from *Aw-STRILE-yuh, mite.*"

*   *   *

A kite string goes into a bar and orders a drink.

"Aren't you a kite string?" asks the bartender. "We don't serve kite strings. Get out of here! Scram!"

The kite string goes outside and tangles himself up until he's just a little ball. He rubs himself against the sidewalk until there are little strands sticking up all over him. Then he goes back into the bar and tries to order another drink.

"Hey," says the bartender, "aren't you that kite string I just threw out?"

"No," says the kite string. "I'm a frayed knot."

8
JUGGLE

> *"How ill white hairs becomes a fool and jester!"*
> —*William Shakespeare*, Henry IV

When my oldest daughter was one, I was her second favorite person in the world. Unfortunately, it was a distant second. Whenever her mother left the house, she would scream and carry on as if she'd been left with a perfect stranger—or maybe a serial killer.

Luckily, after fifteen or twenty minutes she'd figure out that I was her only option, and she'd decide to make the best of it. Before long we'd be laughing and playing, and I'd be the best thing to come along since sliced bread. Then my wife would get back and I'd be chopped liver again.

One day, for reasons I never discovered, the serial killer phase slipped directly into the chopped liver phase, and the crying didn't stop. Thirty minutes. Forty minutes. An hour and a half. I was desperate. I tried funny faces. I tried silly voices. I tried running around with a diaper on my head. Nothing. Not even a smile.

Finally, in a stroke of dumb luck and sheer panic (a parent's two greatest friends), I grabbed some oranges out of the fridge and started to juggle. At first this was no more successful than anything else. But as soon as I dropped one, which didn't take long, I was rewarded with a laugh. I tried it again, this time dropping all three. *Big* laugh. Then I dropped them on my foot and hopped up and down like I was hurt. Bring-down-the-house laugh.

By the time my wife got home, I was just dropping oranges on my head one at a time and collapsing on the floor while my daughter giggled uncontrollably and squealed for more.

"What are you doing?" my wife asked.

"Juggling," I said. "Don't ask."

Of the many graces with which we are blessed as parents, dignity is not one.

WHEN TO START

This is not really a little kid's skill. Most children don't develop the hand-eye coordination to juggle until they're at least seven or eight. Even then there's an important quality that they often lack—patience.

The first steps in learning to juggle are monotonous, but there's no getting around them. Unless your kids have the ability to stay on task and deal with a little delayed gratification, you might want to wait until they're ten or twelve and their improved coordination lets them pick it up quickly. Even then this is a skill that is learned over hours or days, as opposed to minutes.

WHAT TO JUGGLE

The perfect set of objects for learning to juggle would have the following characteristics. All three would have a uniform size, shape, and weight. They would fit comfortably in the palm of the hand. They would be heavy enough to land in your palm with authority, but could be tossed with just a small motion of the wrist. Most important, they wouldn't bounce or roll when they landed in your hand or on the floor.

One thing that meets all these criteria is a beanbag. You can buy beanbags for juggling at many toy stores, but it's just as easy to make a set for yourself. Here's how.

Find three kid-sized socks of equal weight and three small, Ziploc plastic bags. Fill each of the bags with a half cup of dried rice or beans and a few pennies for extra weight. Squeeze the air out of the bags, zip them shut, and fold them into little balls.

Drop a bag into the toe of each sock. Wrap each sock around its bag until there's only a couple of inches left, then turn that last part inside out so it covers the entire ball.

Voilà! Instant beanbags.

BASIC TECHNIQUE

Juggling is both surprisingly simple and maddeningly complex. There is only one small motion involved, repeated again and again with both hands. However, the timing and precision of that motion must be exact. For that reason, your child should be very comfortable with each step in the learning process before he moves on.

Step 1: The throw and catch

This is the basic unit of all juggling. No matter what the objects are, or how many of them are up in the air, each one must travel in a specific arc to a specific spot where it can be caught at a specific time.

Have your child stand with legs a little apart and arms bent at the elbows with palms upturned. His hands should be cupped so a beanbag fits loosely inside.

Have him toss a beanbag back and forth from one hand to the other. Each toss should start at belly-button level and travel in an arc that peaks a few inches above the top of the head. There should be as little motion as possible—only the wrists and forearms should move.

Ideally, every toss travels through the same arc. They peak at the same height in both directions, and they end up very near the other hand so they can be caught without reaching.

It's important to catch and throw with the hand in the same relaxed, cupped position. Most kids have a tendency to grab at the beanbag and squeeze it. Instead, get them to cradle it in their cupped hand when they catch it, then toss it with a scooping motion without ever wrapping their fingers around it.

Once the tosses get more consistent, add a new wrinkle. Have your kids focus straight ahead, seeing the beanbag only at the top of its arc. They should still be able to catch it using their peripheral vision. This will become very important later, when there are three balls to keep track of at once.

As simple as it seems, the toss and catch is absolutely critical. Try to get your kids to practice until it can be done without thinking. Make a game of it to keep their interest. Count consecutive catches without a drop, or challenge them to a head-to-head battle. If you can keep them at it long enough to get consistent, accurate tosses, the rest of your job will be much easier.

Step 2: The exchange

This is the most difficult step. However, once it's mastered, the actual juggling is a breeze.

Again, have your kid stand in a comfortable position with palms upturned. This time, place a beanbag in each hand. Just as before, have him throw one beanbag in an arc to the other hand. As that beanbag reaches the peak of its arc, have him toss the second bag back to the other hand, then catch the first beanbag. For now it's okay to let the second beanbag drop. Have him concentrate on just getting the second toss off in time to catch the first.

At this point you'll notice that if the second toss travels the exact same arc as the first, the bags will collide in midair. To avoid this, the second bag must be tossed just to the inside of the first. In other words, a toss from the right hand to the left travels an arc that's a few inches to the left of tosses in the opposite direction. The two arcs are the same size and shape, but they are shifted a few inches apart (see drawing).

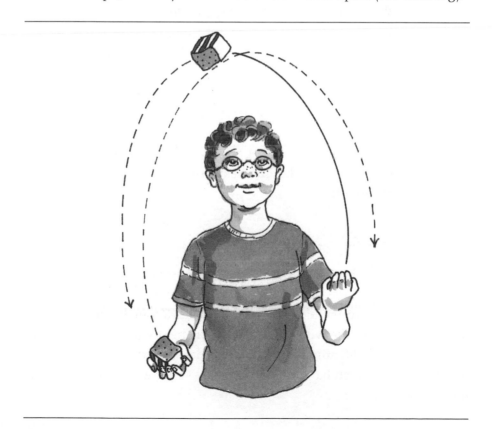

The hardest thing about this exchange is the timing. As the first toss flies through the air, it's easy to panic and unload the second toss too soon. Unfortunately, this would make it virtually impossible to get off a third toss in the proper rhythm, and two consecutive tosses don't really qualify as juggling. The second toss has to wait until the first toss reaches its peak. As long as the hands stay in the same cupped position for both toss and catch, there should be plenty of time to launch the second beanbag and still catch the first.

Once the timing falls into place, work on consistency. There's a tendency to shovel the second beanbag in a low arc to make sure the hand is free to catch the first one. Both tosses should have the same height, and the same accuracy. When the second toss looks like the first, and it ends up in the opposite hand, the exchange is complete.

Have your child practice the exchange from both sides until it's second nature. Make sure he focuses his eyes on the peaks of the tosses, making the catches with his peripheral vision. And just as before, try to keep him at it until he achieves consistency from both sides. Now that there's more than one beanbag involved, a bad toss forces a difficult catch, which in turn makes the next toss even worse. Without consistency, everything falls apart.

Step 3: The juggle

Juggling is nothing more than a series of exchanges. The only difference between three good tosses and three hundred is consistency.

To start, have your child hold two beanbags in one hand and one in the other. On the side with two bags, one is held with the thumb and the index and middle fingers, while the other is cradled in the palm. It doesn't matter which hand holds two bags—choose the side that feels more comfortable.

Starting on the two-bag side, have your kid toss the beanbag that's held with thumb and fingers. He does an exchange as usual, but instead of catching the ball on the other side, he goes directly into a second exchange. Eventually, a third and a fourth will follow.

As in Step 2, pay attention to the shape and position of the arcs. Remember that the tossed beanbag is always released a few inches inside of the one that's about to be caught. This means that the hands actually move in a slight loop: inside and upward to toss, outside and downward to catch. The inside-outside parts are very subtle—just enough to keep the balls from colliding.

At this point there's nothing to add but practice. But don't forget to acknowledge all the work your kid has done so far. Two consecutive exchanges officially qualifies as juggling! Celebration and abundant praise are in order.

TROUBLESHOOTING

Frustration

Juggling can be maddening. It seems so simple—but the least little mistake can start an irreversible cascade that ends in failure.

The first thing to do is get your kid to relax. If you're a beginner too, learn along with him and model patience. Juggling requires a little bit of Zen. You always do better getting into a rhythm and flow than you do trying to will the balls to stay in the air.

The other thing you can try is getting back to basics. Go back to a level of mastery, even if it's just tossing the ball from one hand to the other. Sometimes muscle memory needs a refresher course. Make sure your kid doesn't see it as a setback, though. Let him know it's just a way to find a groove and a rhythm.

Happy Feet

Many people, when they first start to juggle, find themselves lurching around the room, often lunging forward with every throw. This is because reaching forward for one toss causes them to make the next toss with a jabbing motion, and that one goes forward as well. There are several ways to fix this. One is to juggle in front of a wall or a low table. Another is to practice while sitting down. The idea is to toss with more discipline, rather than compensating for poor tosses with the feet.

Bad Timing

Some people just can't be convinced that they can wait until the ball is at its peak and still have enough time to toss another ball and catch the first one. For these people, higher tosses may be the answer. It certainly gives them more time, but it results in less accurate tosses. Once the rhythm is established, it's best to lower the tosses slightly to a more manageable height.

Wild Tosses

If the timing is fine but the tosses still seem to be going all over the place, try tossing a little lower. It provides less time, but it makes the tosses more accurate. It's also useful to imagine that with each toss, the hand is pushing the beanbag up an imaginary tube. This can eliminate excessive motion, especially at the wrists.

WHAT'S NEXT

Once the three-ball juggle is mastered, there's no end to the juggling tricks you can try. Here are three that are about at the next level of skill:

Two-Person Juggling

If two people have about the same level of juggling skill, they can try juggling together. One way to do this is side by side. Basically, one person acts as the left hand and the other acts as the right hand. For some, this is actually easier than regular juggling, because you have to keep track of only one side at a time.

The other way to do it is face to face. Both jugglers stand with two balls in their right hand, about three or four feet apart. They raise their hands together, drop them together, and begin juggling at the same time. After an agreed upon number of tosses, each of them tosses from their right hand to the other juggler's left hand, instead of to their own. Eventually this can be done with every right hand throw.

Outside Cascade

Remember the loops that your hands make when you juggle? If you reverse their direction, you toss the ball from the outside and catch it on the inside. You still avoid midair collisions, but you end up with an effect that makes the balls look like they're cascading down like a waterfall. This juggle has the same rhythm as the normal three-ball juggle, but the motion feels less natural. Still, with a little practice it's not hard to learn.

Sticks and Pins

Any elongated object can be juggled, but some have a balance that makes them much easier. Juggling pins are especially designed for juggling, and they're a good place to start.

The only difference between pins and balls is the rotation. A pin needs to rotate a specific number of times on every toss, so the handle is in the right place when you catch it. (The importance of this will become apparent when you move on to torches and knives.)

You can learn to juggle pins using the same steps as with balls, getting consistency not only with height and accuracy, but with the number of rotations in the air. You'll start out with just one rotation per toss, but eventually you can increase the number as much as you like, as long as it's consistent for each toss.

JUGGLING SCIENCE

How come you can catch a beanbag without actually watching it into your hand? There are two factors involved here—one physical and one biological.

Trajectory

The first factor is a principle known as trajectory. When you launch an object into the air at a certain speed and angle, it will always travel through the same arc and land in the same place. This is why medieval armies could catapult rocks into enemy fortresses. What's more, the part of the arc that comes before the peak will look just like the part that comes after the peak. Of course, a feather or a paper airplane won't follow this rule, but a ball on a windless day will.

When you see a juggling ball at the peak of its arc, your brain gets all the information it needs to calculate where the ball will land. It knows what the ball did in the first part of its arc, so it can tell what it will do in the second part. Of course, you don't have to think this through and do all the calculations. Your brain does it for you in a split second, then moves your hand into the right position to make the catch.

Try this. Stand a few feet from your child and play catch with a beanbag. Now, try closing your eyes right as the beanbag reaches its peak. You'll be amazed at how many throws you're still able to catch.

Peripheral Vision

When you're trying to catch a juggling ball, your brain has another trick up its sleeve. It's called peripheral vision.

At the back of our eyeball is the surface that senses light and allows us to see, called the retina. There are many different kind of sensors in the retina. The ones in the middle allow us to see color and detail. When we are looking directly at something, these are the sensors we use. But on the outside of the retina there are sensors that pick up light from the edges of our vision. This is called our peripheral vision.

With our peripheral vision, we don't see color and detail very well, but we can do other things. For instance, we can pick up very dim light, which is why it's easier to see faint stars when you don't look right at them. But the other thing we can do is see motion.

Try this. Stand directly behind your child and have him close his eyes. On either side of his head, hold out a finger so it points forward, with its tip about a foot from his ear. You may have to play around with the position to find the edge of his peripheral vision.

Now have him open his eyes. If he looks straight forward, he won't be able to see your fingertips. But if you move them, the fingers will suddenly come into view. With our peripheral vision, we see moving objects much better than still ones. This ability probably evolved to pick up stalking predators, but it also works on juggling balls.

JUGGLING RECORDS

The record for most balls juggled at once is somewhat clouded by undocumented claims. Reports of eleven-ball juggling have been made, but none documented in a continuous pattern. The record for ten-ball juggling is twenty-two catches, held by Bruce Sarafian. But for nine-ball juggling, the number jumps to seventy-eight documented catches by Anthony Gatto, who is said to do up to two hundred catches in practice.

For three-ball juggling, the endurance record is six hours, twenty-six minutes, thirty-one seconds, held by Dave Pope and Jas Angelo of Great Britain.

STUPID JUGGLING JOKES

Q: What has three heads, looks really goofy, and knows how to juggle?

A: Oh, I forgot, you don't have three heads.

*   *   *

A little boy was walking down the street when he came across a street performer setting up his act. The man put out a sign that read: WILL JUGGLE ANYTHING—ONE DOLLAR.

"If I gave you a dollar, would you really juggle *anything?*" asked the boy.

"Pretty much," said the performer. "What do you have in mind?"

"How about my baby brother?"

The man laughed. "What if I dropped him?" he asked.

"Well," said the boy, "I could give you a dollar fifty, but that's all I've got."

9
BUILD A FIRE

"Darkness cannot drive out darkness;
only light can do that.
Hate cannot drive out hate;
only love can do that."

—Martin Luther King Jr.

Once, when I was a kid, a big November storm took us by surprise. We watched the dark clouds roll in over the mountains and spread across the sky. The wind rose quickly and whipped at the tall trees on either side of our yard. Soon, sheets of rain rattled our big picture window, and my dad called us away from the glass, afraid it might break.

My mom was about to start dinner when the electricity went out, and we were plunged into darkness. Usually, something so exciting and unexpected would have had us running around the house with glee, but the ominous sounds of the storm, coupled with my parents' anxiety, kept us all a little subdued.

My father lit some candles and built a fire in the fireplace. He said the lights would come back on any minute. We waited quietly, listening to the roar of the storm. Nothing happened.

An hour or so later we started getting hungry. My dad found some crackers in the cupboard, but that didn't help much. Then my mom came out of the kitchen and knelt down in front of the fireplace. She had four cans of baked beans, a sack of potatoes, and a canned ham. We all watched in amazement as she opened up the top of the cans, wrapped the potatoes in tin foil, and used the fireplace tongs to put everything in the fire.

It was the best dinner we ever had. My brothers and I still talked about it years later. We never knew food could taste so good.

About halfway through the meal the lights came back on. My parents were obviously relieved. They immediately began putting out candles and taking food back to the kitchen where it belonged. But we were disappointed. We pleaded with my parents to let us pretend that the electricity was still off.

My father laughed and shook his head. He was a practical man, not given to many fantasies or imaginings of his own. He wasn't the kind who, simply on the whim of his children, would waste a perfectly good evening sitting in the dark. At least, that's what we thought.

He shook his head one more time, then walked across the room and turned out the lights.

WHEN TO START

This is not a difficult skill, at least as far as technique. Once you understand the basic principles, it's no harder than playing with Lincoln Logs. The biggest issue when you teach it to kids isn't their physical ability, it's their emotional maturity.

Fire has the power to bewitch, and that's especially true for kids. Every child is a potential pyromaniac until proven otherwise. Make sure your kids have the judgment and self-control to treat a fire with respect—both for their own safety and everyone else's.

BASIC PRINCIPLES

Every fire requires three things: oxygen, fuel, and heat. If any one of these is missing, the fire won't burn, but a short supply of one can be balanced out by a surplus of the others.

When you first start a fire, there is very little heat, so you need good fuel and lots of oxygen. The first thing you light should be highly flammable and exposed to the air. This usually means something dry, with lots of surface area, like paper. As the fire burns, it makes more heat. Now it can ignite fuel that has less surface area, like sticks. Finally, as the fire gets very hot, it can consume large chunks of fuel that burn for a long time. In other words: logs.

This progression is the same no matter where you build your fire. Start with small, fast-burning fuel and let the fire move on to larger, slower fuel. At every step, make sure the fuel is dry and that there's plenty of air. Follow these rules and you are guaranteed success.

FIREPLACE FIRES

There's nothing like a roaring fire in the fireplace to make your whole house feel cozy and warm. And there's nothing like setting off the fire alarm, and opening your windows in December to let the smoke out, to ruin your whole day. This isn't rocket science, but it's worth learning to do it right.

WHAT YOU NEED BEFORE YOU START

Equipment

Basic fireplace tools include some tongs or a poker to reposition logs, a small shovel to move ashes, and a brush to deal with stray sparks or embers. A pair of heavy leather gloves comes in handy for adding fresh wood to the fire. Some people use a small bellows to help get the fire started, but your lungs or a newspaper fan will work just as well.

The fireplace itself should be equipped with a screen or door to contain sparks and a heavy metal grate to help circulate air beneath the logs. There should be a fire extinguisher in the room, but don't expose it to direct heat from the fire.

Finally, you'll need matches. The long wooden ones are safer and easier, especially if your child does the lighting. A short match and a long candle will do the same thing.

Fuel

For tinder, meaning something to light, you can use newspaper. If there's none available, almost any paper will do, but avoid burning too much glossy paper or colored ink, both of which release chemicals during combustion.

You'll also want plenty of kindling. This can be as simple as a bunch of dry sticks and twigs, but it can also be a wood with flammable resins, like cedar or Georgia Fatwood, which is sold in little bundles specifically for starting fires.

For firewood you'll want logs or pieces in a variety of sizes, from about one inch in diameter to six inches and beyond. Split and dried (or seasoned) wood is the best. Hardwoods like oak, maple, alder, and cherry will burn the longest and the hottest. Softwoods like pine and fir burn more quickly and leave a residue on the inside of the chimney. This means more frequent visits from the chimney sweep to prevent chimney fires (see below). Never use wood that has been painted, varnished, finished, or treated—these can release noxious fumes when burned, and they may pose a serious health threat.

BASIC TECHNIQUE

Step 1: Prepare the hearth

As soon as you even *think* about building a fire in your fireplace, open the flue. Do it right away, before you have a chance to forget. There's nothing more embarrassing than getting smoked out of your home by your own stupidity. You end up standing in your robe and pajamas, flapping the front door to clear the smoke while your neighbors point and laugh. Not that *I've* ever done it, mind you...

The flue handle may stick out of the fireplace wall, or you may have to reach up into the chimney. Some open with a push or a pull, and some with a twist. Occasionally, a chimney will have no flue at all. The only way to be sure is to get down on your knees and look up there with a flashlight. The difference between open and closed may be only a few inches, so check it with the handle in both positions. But don't fiddle with the handle while your head is still underneath, or you'll end up looking like Al Jolson.

Once the flue is open, remove the ashes from under the grate to create an air space. Make sure your tools, spark screen, extra firewood, and fire extinguisher are all within reach.

Step 2: Build the fire

Loosely crumple a few sheets of newspaper and stuff them under the grate. Don't pack them too tight—you want plenty of air down there. Make sure they stick out from under the grate so you can light them easily. If you don't have a grate, make your own by putting a log on either side of the fireplace and laying three or four sturdy sticks across them.

On top of the grate, put a generous pile of kindling. Leave spaces between the sticks that are as wide as the sticks themselves. Don't skimp—this stuff burns up fast, and you want it to burn long enough to ignite the larger pieces.

Place a layer of small logs, an inch or so in diameter, at right angles to the kindling. Again, leave some space in between the pieces. Finally, put one or two larger pieces on top of the pile. Resist the temptation to use more than that at first—large logs will smother a fire unless there's sufficient heat to keep it going.

Finally, check to make sure the entire structure is stable. The last thing you need is a flaming log rolling onto your living room rug when the pile beneath it collapses.

Step 3: Lighting it

With a long match or candle, light the newspaper under the grate. Light as many spots as you can, starting at the back and working your way forward. Once the paper has ignited the kindling, use a bellows, a magazine, or your lungs to gently fan the flames. A cardboard tube—from a roll of paper towels or wrapping paper—will concentrate your breath and direct it where it's needed.

Step 4: Care and feeding

Once your fire is lit, wait until the bigger pieces of wood are burning nicely before you add any more. Each new log should be placed at an angle to the ones beneath it, so air can circulate between them.

Never leave a fire unattended without a screen in front of it. When you go to sleep for the night, separate the logs and push them to the back of the fireplace. In the morning, don't forget to close the flue—it conserves heat and keeps the birds out.

CAMPFIRES

If the hearth is the soul of any home, the fire pit is the soul of your campsite. Building a fire is a little trickier outdoors, but the basic idea is the same.

WHAT YOU NEED BEFORE YOU START

Equipment

You won't need anything fancy. Bring a small shovel, like a hand trowel, and a small ax or handsaw. Have a bucket of water handy at all times. You'll need a box of dry matches, and I'd recommend a disposable lighter in case the wind keeps blowing out your matches. Finally, you might want to bring a couple of fire-starting sticks just for insurance. These are made of compressed sawdust and wax, and they're a big help when there's no dry tinder. I know—it's cheating. But it's better to swallow your pride than to have a campout without a proper fire.

Choosing a Site

For obvious reasons, you can't just build a fire wherever you like. Campgrounds, state and national parks, and national forests allow campfires only in certain locations. There may also be times of year when open fires are banned entirely, due to the high risk of forest fires. Unless you're absolutely sure, ask.

Most of the time, you'll be building your campfire in an established fire circle. But not all circles are created equal. The ideal spot is shielded from the wind, near a source of water, and surrounded by rock or bare dirt. There should be a buffer zone of at least three feet on all sides, and there should be no overhanging branches.

If you're out in the middle of nowhere and you have to make your own fire circle, try to find a rocky streamside or a gravely beach. If that isn't possible, locate a spot where the ground is mostly bare dirt. Clear all flammable material from a circle about eight feet in diameter. In the center of that area, make a smaller circle out of large stones. If none are available, dig a pit about two feet in diameter and six inches deep.

Fuel

You'll need tinder, kindling, and firewood, just as you did in your fireplace. The key is that everything has to be dry. Don't even think about using anything live or green.

Dry leaves, thin bark, or dry pine needles all make good tinder. If none of these are available, crumpled paper works fine. For kindling, choose small, dry sticks about a quarter inch in diameter.

You'll need firewood in a variety of sizes. If you can purchase firewood or bring it with you, it'll make things a lot easier, but you'll still need a bunch of sticks about an inch in diameter to get the fire going. These can be gathered from the ground or split from your larger pieces.

BASIC TECHNIQUE

Step 1: Build the fire

Make a little pile of tinder in the center of your pit. Don't wad it up too tight. Remember, you need air. Over the tinder, make a little teepee with your kindling. Make sure the sides of the teepee are in contact with the tinder.

Now, around the teepee, build a box out of your one-inch-diameter sticks. Place a stick on either side, touching the base of the teepee. Put two more sticks on the next level at 90-degree angles to the first two.

Notice that as you go up, the walls of the box slant inward to stay in contact with the teepee. Once your box is done, take three or four larger sticks and make an outer teepee, leaning them against each other and against the sides of the box. Be gentle—you don't want to knock the whole thing down.

Step 2: Lighting it

Using your body as a shield against the wind, light a match. Cup your hand around it to keep it lit, and light the tinder at the center of the inner teepee. If there's a lot of wind, try to shield the fire until the kindling teepee starts to ignite. If there's no wind at all, blow gently or fan the fire until the flames really get going.

Step 3: Care and feeding

Don't add new wood too soon. Make sure the fire is really going and some hot coals have formed that can ignite a larger piece of wood. Take one end of the log and place it at the edge of the fire. Then, using another stick as a tool, lower the other end of the log until it leans on the pieces that are already burning.

Step 4: Putting it out

Every year, forest fires start as a result of simple carelessness. When you're ready to go to bed, put the fire out, and do it completely. Carefully douse it with water a little at a time, being very careful to avoid the ashes and hot steam that erupt when water meets hot coals. Once the fire is out, mix it with a stick and add more water. Shovel some dirt on top, and mix that in as well. Remember that a coal or ember can remain hot for many hours, even when there are no visible sparks or flames. Your goal is to deprive the fire of all oxygen. When all the smoke is gone, add a final layer of dirt and pack it down firmly.

TROUBLESHOOTING

The Fire Won't Light

This is pretty much an outdoor problem, unless you're trying to light a fireplace fire with wet newspaper. Wind is the usual culprit. Try your best to shield the match, and if that doesn't work, use the disposable lighter as a fallback. If the match stays lit but the tinder doesn't, make sure it's dry enough. If there isn't dry tinder available, the fire-starting stick should do the trick, as long as the kindling isn't wet too.

The Fire Doesn't Stay Lit

If your tinder ignites but your kindling or your firewood doesn't, there are several possible causes. Again, make sure everything is dry. Also make sure you've built the fire with layers of wood that increase gradually in size. Quarter-inch kindling will ignite one-inch branches, but it won't burn long enough to ignite a full-sized log.

If the size and quality of your fuel is okay, the problem must be in the heat or the oxygen. Check the spacing of your logs. If they are right up against one another, no air can circulate, and the fire will suffocate. On the other hand, if they're too far apart, the heat of one log can't help sustain the heat of the others. Keep larger logs about an inch apart. This allows flames to rise between the two surfaces, burning them both at the same time.

Smoke Gets in Your Eyes

If smoke comes billowing out of the fireplace and into your house, it could mean any one of several problems.

If you suddenly realize that you never checked the flue, and the handle is inside the chimney, put the fire out with your fire extinguisher. Don't try to reach up and open the flue unless the flames are still small and the smoke is manageable.

Sometimes a chimney draws poorly because it's filled with cold air. Since cold air is heavier than warm air, it wants to sink down into your house. To reverse this flow, light a roll of newspaper and hold it as high as you can get it in the chimney. This will create enough heat to make the air rise, and the smoke should go up instead of down. They make all kinds of fancy chimney caps to help your chimney draw, but the newspaper trick is a lot cheaper, and it works surprisingly well.

Snap, Crackle, Pop

Wet wood, or soft wood with flammable resins, may pop and crackle when it gets really hot. Although kids find this very entertaining, it creates some problems. The tiny explosions can send hot sparks and embers in any direction. The best strategy here is vigilance. If you're indoors, keep the screen up, and keep a brush handy. Outdoors, make sure everyone keeps their distance, and track any embers that fly beyond the nonflammable area you cleared.

COOK-INS AND COOKOUTS

It's a proven kid-fact that anything tastes better when it's cooked over an open fire. Campfire meals can be as simple or elaborate as you like, but you'll want to follow certain rules.

First of all, don't cook over a roaring fire. The flames are unpredictable, and they tend to scorch the food, the cookware, and the chef's arms. In general, you should either cook beside the fire or over red-hot coals.

Before you build your fire, prepare a little area that is connected to the main fire circle but is also surrounded by rocks. Make the rocks the same height, so a grating will lie across them without tipping. After the fire has turned several large logs into embers, sweep some of the larger coals into your cooking area with a stick. You can adjust the temperature by adding or subtracting coals, or by moving the food on and off the heat as needed. Cast iron cookware is best, since it's nearly indestructible and already black.

If you're having an indoor cookout, or if you don't want to bother with pots and pans, you can just keep it simple. Give everyone a long skewer and let them cook their own sausage, hot dog, or shish kebob. You'll want to use oven mitts or wrap towels around little hands so they don't get too hot. Consider precooking your meat, so you can just brown it without worrying about cooking it through. Canned foods, like baked beans or ham, can be moved in and out of the fire with oven mitts and tongs. You can wrap potatoes in three layers of foil and drop them right in the coals. Just check them once in a while so they don't burn.

Of course, for dessert there's s'mores! For the uninitiated, these are sandwiches made from graham crackers, chocolate bars, and hot toasted marshmallows. They are way too sweet and way too messy. In other words, they're a kid's idea of heaven.

SAFETY TIPS

Follow These Rules

1. No kid lights a match, a candle, a lighter, or anything else without a grown-up.
2. No kid touches, manipulates, or feeds the fire in any way without a grown-up's okay.
3. Once it's lit, the fire is never left unattended.
4. Before you go to sleep, indoor fires are contained and outdoor fires are put out.
5. All kids are pyromaniacs. Expect them to break the rules.

First Aid

The treatment of minor burns is very simple: immediately plunge the burn into the coldest water you can find and leave it there for as long as you can—preferably at least five minutes. This limits the tissue damage and inflammation. If your kids get burned, they won't want to put their hand into ice water that long. Tough. Make them do it.

If the burn blisters up, wrap it to keep it clean and get the child to a doctor within the next day or so. If it's larger than an inch or two, bring her to the doctor right away. If there's no blistering, you can probably just watch it and treat it as you would a sunburn.

Smoke Inhalation

Smoke is toxic. Most deaths in house fires are the result of smoke inhalation rather than burns. At a campfire, always sit upwind to the fire. If the wind is shifting, keep your distance so the smoke can rise before it gets to you. And if your chimney isn't drawing well, either fix the problem or put out the fire. All of this goes double if someone in the family has asthma.

Chimney Fires

When wood burns, it releases particles in its smoke that coat the inside of your chimney. This residue is called creosote. Soft, resinous woods like pine, cedar, and fir lay down more creosote than hardwoods, but they all deposit some. When it builds up enough, it can actually ignite and turn your chimney into a roaring inferno. The resulting heat will almost certainly start a house fire.

The best defense against chimney fires is prevention. Have a chimney sweep clean out your chimney about once every fifty fires, especially if you burn soft wood. If you are ever burning a fire and there's a roar, a shake, or a vibration in the chimney, accompanied by smoke in the house or hot spots on the wall, evacuate the house immediately and call 911.

FIRE IN THE BELLY

Every time you warm your hands by a roaring fire, you're actually feeling the warmth of the sun. By that I mean that the energy released from the wood was stored there by capturing the energy of the sun's rays. In a process called photosynthesis (see *Chapter 4: Plant a Tree*), the tree used the sun's energy to combine water from the ground with carbon dioxide from the air, making wood.

When we make a fire, we reverse that process. The wood is combined with oxygen and broken down into carbon dioxide and water vapor, which are released into the air. The stored-up energy is also released—as heat.

Fire isn't the only form of combustion. The food we eat also has stored energy from photosynthesis. Our cells break down the food into water and carbon dioxide, releasing the energy we need to survive. But in order to do this, our cells must combine the food with oxygen. That's why people—and fires—need to breathe.

FIRE-STARTING QUIZ

Now that you've read this chapter and studied it thoroughly, you're ready for a pop quiz.

Imagine that you are trapped in a strange room in complete darkness. You have a matchbox, but there's only one match left. You grope around the room and find a newspaper, a pile of sticks, and a candle. Which do you light first?

(*Answer: The match.*)

10
MAKE A SAND CASTLE

> *"Build on, and make thy castles high and fair,*
> *Rising and reaching upward to the skies;*
> *Listen to voices in the upper air,*
> *Nor lose thy simple faith in mysteries."*
> —Henry Wadsworth Longfellow

When we were kids, the problem we had with sand castles was that the results never lived up to our expectations. We'd set out to construct a medieval fortress and end up with a squat little lump, collapsing from the weight of its own towers. We tried it once at the beginning of each vacation, then moved on to something with a better chance of success.

One summer we were playing on the beach when an old man appeared, pulling a rusty red wagon full of junk. I'm not really sure how old he was, but to us he seemed ancient—at least over fifty. He parked his wagon where the asphalt met the soft sand and began to carry his stuff down to the edge of the water, a few objects at a time. They were beat-up, old containers of various sizes, each one with its bottom cut off. We stopped what we were doing to watch him. It was that rare anomaly—a grown-up doing something interesting.

We watched with rapt attention as he proceeded to build the largest sand castle we'd ever seen. It was almost as tall as he was. And it wasn't just big, it was palatial! The sand held together magically as he carved its elaborate details: ramparts, guard houses, watchtowers, and stairs.

By the time he had finished, we overcame our shyness. We gathered around and peppered him with questions. He answered each one patiently, and then he said that he had to go. But he left us a gift: the battered, bottomless containers that were the key to his magic.

"Go ahead—they're yours," he said. "I was gonna make new ones soon anyway."

That summer we made castle after castle, each one larger and more splendid than the last. We never got tired of it. Finally, we could make them big enough to fit our dreams.

WHEN TO START

Some kids love to build. Some kids love to destroy. Woe to the parent with one of each.

Young kids are often the destroyers, and in their presence sand castles have a limited life expectancy. If you're working with little ones, build quickly, then sit back and enjoy watching them take entropy into their own hands. But if you also have an older child who wants to create a beachfront Taj Mahal, set up a separate construction site where the younger child can practice his demolition skills.

WHAT YOU NEED BEFORE YOU START

Sand

Of course, your best option is the beach, but not all beaches are created equal. What you're looking for is fine sand that sticks together and holds its shape when it's wet. It should also be relatively clean. Too many rocks, shells, or seaweed will break up its cohesiveness.

If there are no beaches nearby, a sandbox is a suitable replacement. It should have good drainage, because you're going to add a lot of water. You'll need to buy some extra sand if you want to make a good-sized castle. The fine, white sand sold as "play sand" is ideal, but cheaper, construction-grade sand will work.

Shovel

For a big castle, use a garden spade. For a smaller one, a plastic scoop or hand trowel will do.

Bucket

You'll want at least a two-gallon pail to bring water up from the surf. If you're building in a sandbox, a garden hose and a faucet will save your back, and a lot of time.

Building Molds

To make the basic structure for your castle, you'll need a series of plastic containers in different sizes. For really big castles, you can even start with a garbage can, followed by smaller trash cans, buckets, and yogurt or cottage cheese containers. Smooth sides make it easier to remove the molds from the packed sand—avoid containers with horizontal ridges.

Each container will form one story of your castle, and its diameter should be a couple of inches smaller than the one below it. Cut the bottom off each one to make a cylinder, then smooth any sharp edges or cover them with duct tape.

Carving Tools

Often, these can be fashioned from driftwood right at the beach. However, it's worth bringing a spatula or a pie server to smooth surfaces and to cut straight edges. Plastic eating utensils also come in handy. For fine details you'll need something sharp, like a pencil, and a plastic straw to blow away excess sand. If more than one child will be working at once, bring enough tools for everyone.

Spray Vegetable Oil, or WD-40

Optional, for coating molds so they can be removed more easily.

BASIC TECHNIQUE

Step 1: Select a building site

Once you've located a beach with the right kind of sand, find out what the tide is doing. An outgoing tide leaves the sand nice and wet, and you can start building right next to the water so you won't be hauling buckets all day.

If the tide is coming in, make sure you give yourself enough room to account for the rising water. Some kids love to watch the waves consume their creation, but for others it's traumatic. Try to gauge this before you begin, and choose your spot accordingly. If you start building at high tide, your castle will be above the high-water mark. As it dries, it will crumble slowly over many hours, and look like an ancient ruin.

A beach with a gradual slope has several advantages. There are usually tide pools to provide water far from the waves, and the incoming tide is fast and dramatic. If you build the castle on a large mound, it will become an island fortress as the water flows around it.

Step 2: Make a hill

A proper castle should be sited on a hill to give a commanding view of the kingdom. This also gives it a little more protection from toddlers and incoming waves.

Pile up some sand with your shovel, and make a large crater on top. Fill the crater with water, and stomp it down until the sand is packed into a firm foundation. Pile on some more sand, and repeat until you have a hill of the proper dimensions to support your first story.

Step 3: Fill the molds

For easy removal later, you can coat your molds with a thin layer of vegetable oil or WD-40, but do it while they're still dry. Take your largest, bottomless container and place it upside down on your mound. Fill it to the top with sand and water, alternating between the two and packing it down as you go. As you work, there should be standing water at the top. Reach in and push down the sand from the top. Better yet, lift up your kids and have them stomp around for a while. The key here is to make the sand very wet and to compress it as tightly as possible to remove all air spaces and pockets of dry sand.

Once the first container is filled, stack the next largest one right on top of it and repeat the process. Make sure you aren't making the Leaning Tower of Pisa. Keep going until the smallest container is sitting on top.

Once all the containers are stacked and full, and the standing water has drained away, remove the molds from the top down. The top stories may come off as you remove their molds. Just push the container back down to repack them a little, then continue.

The larger containers can be difficult to remove, so be patient. Work your fingers under the rim and lift a little at a time. Once the seal between the mold and the sand is broken, it should come off easily. Take care not to disturb the upper stories while you remove the lower molds.

Step 4: Start carving

There's no end to what you can do with good sand and a lot of patience. Start at the top and work your way down, so the sand you carve away doesn't land on finished sections. Turrets, windows, battlements, stairways—let your inner medieval architect go wild.

For fine details, clear away discarded sand by blowing gently through a straw. To add landscaping, try creating hedges and trees by dripping very soupy sand off the ends of your fingertips. The drips will pile up into weird shapes, and if you concentrate a narrow stream over one spot they'll form peaks (see drawing).

Step 5: Final touches

Use shells and seaweed and beach glass to adorn your creation. Build little driftwood soldiers and erect candy wrapper flags. Use crabs and clams as sentries, or as monsters lurking in the moat.

You can use your molds to create monuments and sculptures on the castle grounds. I like to break out of the strict, medieval mode. Our last castle was surrounded by giant Easter Island tiki heads, a pyramid, a sphinx, and a lopsided Arc de Triomphe. And don't forget the surrounding kingdom. What's a castle without feudal peasants?

If the tide is coming in, build a moat around the base of the hill. It makes for added drama when the waves advance and keeps your castle standing a few moments longer. An overturned sandal makes a great drawbridge, but don't forget to extract it before you go home.

WHAT COMES NEXT?

Once you've mastered a basic castle, there's a whole world of sand carving to explore. The technique is more or less the same—wet, compress, and carve. You're limited only by your imagination.

Many beach communities have yearly sand carving festivals. These are great places to find inspiration. Look on the Internet or call your nearest beach town Chamber of Commerce to see if there's one near you.

SAFETY TIPS

Make sure your kids understand that the ocean is not a big swimming pool. Rushing waves can sweep your feet out from under you even in shallow water. Riptides kill dozens of people every year, even good swimmers. When in doubt, keep everyone out of the water.

Another health threat at the beach is the sun. Excessive sun exposure in childhood is the main cause of skin cancer in adulthood, including the lethal form known as melanoma. Sun block of at least SPF-15 is a must for all but the darkest-skinned kids.

One more problem that's bound to come up is sand in the eyes. When it happens, it's important not to rub. That can drag the sand across the cornea, causing painful abrasions. The best treatment is to irrigate the eye with a saline solution, like the one used to clean contact lenses. If that isn't available, use fresh tap water. Hold the eye open and pour it in. That's no one's idea of a good time, but it's better than leaving sand in the eye.

HOW TO ESCAPE FROM QUICKSAND

When you go down to the edge of the surf to get water, notice how the sand feels under your feet. If you just stand there and wiggle your toes, you'll sink in as if it were a thick liquid. But when you try to pull your foot out quickly, it grabs at you for a second and holds you fast.

This is what quicksand does, only more so. Quicksand is a very thick mixture of fine particles suspended in water, called a colloidal suspension. When you step into it, the particles slide past one another, and you slip into it as you would any liquid. But if you try to move the particles rapidly, they don't have time to get out of each other's way, and they resist you like a solid. That's why, the next time you happen to fall into quicksand, you should swim through it slowly, rather than struggle and thrash about.

You can make your own colloidal suspension by mixing cornstarch and water into a strange substance called "ooblick." Start with a cup of cornstarch in a bowl, and mix in water until it's completely saturated. If you pick some up in your hands, it should run through your fingers and drip down just like a liquid. But if you poke your finger into it quickly, it will suddenly turn into a solid.

Try squeezing together a ball of it and tossing it rapidly back and forth between your hands. As long as you keep it moving, it's a solid ball. When you stop, it dissolves before your eyes.

THE WORLD'S LARGEST SAND CASTLE

In San Diego, California, in September 1997, Gerry Kirk and eighty other sand artists constructed a six-story sand castle entitled the Lost City of Atlantis. It included sea monster sentries and leaping dolphin courtiers, all serving the castle's ruler: Poseidon, the Greek god of the sea.

When finished, the sculpture was more than twenty yards tall and 145 yards wide, and it contained more than 100,000 tons of sand. The work took weeks to complete, and it was stabilized by a sprayed-on coating of Elmer's Glue and water to protect it from wind and rain.

HOW MANY GRAINS OF SAND ARE THERE?

Well, nobody has actually counted them, but here's an educated guess. Mathematicians at the University of Hawaii estimate that on all the beaches in the entire world, there are approximately 7,500,000,000,000,000,000 grains of sand. If you want to say it out loud, that's seven quintillion five quadrillion grains.

STUPID BEACH JOKES

Q: Why is the beach the best place for a picnic?
A: Because of all the *sand-which-is* there.

Q: Why do seagulls fly over the sea?
A: Because if they flew over the bay, they'd be *bagels*.

Q: Why does the ocean roar?
A: You would too, if you had lobsters on your bottom.

11
PLAY A BLADE OF GRASS

*"A song of the good green grass! A song no more of the
city streets; A song of farms—a song of the soil of fields."*
—*Walt Whitman*, Leaves of Grass

The summer before I entered medical school, I scraped together
my meager savings and flew to Europe with a pack on my back
and a rail pass in my pocket. I spent the first leg of my trip wandering the British Isles, going from hostel to hostel, enjoying my freedom while it lasted.

One day, I took a train to Scotland on a whim. I set out with no clear
purpose in mind, but on the way I concocted one. I would visit Loch
Ness. I would search for the monster.

The hostel was a homey, dumpy little place with metal bunk beds
and a jovial manager named Donald. When I asked him for directions
to the Loch, he told me there were three other guests who might like
to join me—a pair of young Japanese students and a German woman,
none of whom spoke much English. We rented all four of the hostel's
rusty bicycles and set off to find Nessie.

Along the way, we got lost twice and had one bicycle break down,
but somehow we made it. We managed to communicate surprisingly
well, using improvised sign language, a little English, and even a little
French. By the time we got to the lake, we felt like comrades.

We all sat down on a grassy hill and pulled out our lunches. The day
was misty and gray, and there was a chill in the air. I picked a blade of

grass and played it like a reed, sending out a long, mournful cry across the Loch. My companions were astonished. None of them had seen this done before. I showed them how, and soon we were all giggling and wailing away.

"We call the monster!" said one of my new Japanese friends. And so we did. All afternoon we ate and laughed and played our blades of grass, waiting for Nessie to appear. Once or twice we were sure we saw her—breaking the surface . . . cocking her ear . . . listening to our strange and mournful calls.

WHEN TO START

This skill is simplicity itself. There's no preparation, no special equipment, no safety issues, and no real purpose. All you need are a pair of thumbs, some long grass (preferably obtained by neglecting to mow your lawn), and a long, lazy summer afternoon.

It does take a little dexterity to hold the blade of grass with just the right amount of tension. Most kids will have some success by around age seven or eight.

BASIC TECHNIQUE

Step 1

Find a long blade of grass—at least an inch or two longer than your thumbs, and about an eighth- to a quarter-inch wide. The thickness and width of the blade will determine its strength, its pitch, and its tone. The blade should be as flat as possible. If it's a wide blade that bends at the central spine that runs down the middle, split it in half and take the flatter side.

Step 2

Put your hands together as if you're praying, and bring your thumbs together, side by side. Keep your hands cupped to create a hollow space between your palms.

Your thumbs should touch in two places: up by the nails and farther down at the bases. Between these two spots there should be a long, narrow opening, like a crevice. This is where you will blow. The idea is to gently stretch the blade of grass from the top of this space to the bottom so it runs straight down the middle.

If the space between your thumbs is less than a quarter inch wide, push together the pinky sides of your palms and turn your thumbs so the nails face slightly away from each other. This should widen the space. You can make it even wider by bending your thumbs.

Step 3

Now, hold one end of the blade of grass between the bases of the thumbs, and the other end between the thumbs where they touch. Start with the thumbs bent slightly, then straighten them to tighten the blade. Don't pull it too tight or you'll break it. It should stretch right down the middle of the space, and you should see only its edge.

Step 4

Open your lips and place them over the opening, nestling them into the hollow between your thumbs. Your lips should be very close to the blade of grass—you may even feel it vibrate as you blow. Blow gently at first, increasing the flow of air gradually until you get the sound you want.

TROUBLESHOOTING

No Sound

Check to make sure the grass blade is stretched tight and that it runs down the middle of the space so air can pass on either side. Adjust the thumbs so the space between them is about a quarter-inch wide.

Broken Blades

If your grass suddenly starts to make a rattling sound, check to see if you've torn the edge. Try to stretch the blade just enough to pull it taut, but not enough to break it. Also, blow as gently as you can and still produce a sound. If, despite all this, the grass continues to break, look around for grass with sturdier blades.

MASTERS' CLASS

Okay, now you're ready for the really advanced stuff. There are lots of ways to vary the sound you get from a blade of grass. First of all, you can experiment with grasses of different thickness and width. Thinner, more delicate blades will give you a higher pitch, and wide ones can sound almost like a honking goose. You can also vary the tension on the grass by wiggling your thumbs. Bending them loosens the blade and lowers the pitch. Don't bend too much—even slight changes in tension have a big effect.

You can create all kinds of sound effects by changing your breath. Try using short, explosive bursts of breath (like saying "too—too—too"), or vibrating your tongue against the roof of your mouth, as if you were saying a rolled, Spanish R.

Finally, try cupping your hands into a ball instead of placing them palm-to-palm. This creates a sound chamber that you can open and close by flapping the fingers of one hand like a door. This produces a "wah—wah—wah" sound, like a train whistle or a trombone. You don't have to move the fingers much to get the effect—just a little flutter will do.

SOME FACTS ABOUT GRASS

- The average cow can eat more than a hundred pounds of grass every day. (Maybe it's time to trade in your lawn mower.)
- A regulation football field (including end zones) contains about twenty million blades of grass.
- There are many species of grass in the world, and they come in all shapes and sizes. The most impressive are in the bamboo family. The largest bamboo can reach a height of more than a hundred feet, and they may be as thick as a foot in diameter. Some of these are among the fastest growing plants in the world, gaining as much as three feet of height in a single day!

THE REED IN YOUR THROAT

As you experiment, you may notice that your grass blades can sound like certain musical instruments—especially saxophones, oboes, clarinets, and bassoons. These are the reed instruments. They get their sound from a thin reed that vibrates as air moves across its edge—just like air blown across a blade of grass.

You may also notice that some of the noises you make sound almost like a human voice. That's because you and I are reed instruments too! The reeds in our throats are thin membranes of tough tissue called vocal cords. When we want to make noise, we bring them together and breathe out so air moves across their edges. This makes them vibrate, and they produce sound.

When the muscles in our throats tighten our vocal cords, the vibrations are faster and the sound has a higher pitch. When we loosen them, the vibrations are slower and the pitch goes down. This is exactly what happens when we tighten or loosen our blades of grass.

When you have a cold, or when you yell and scream too much, your vocal cords get irritated and they thicken. What happens to your voice then? And what happens when we play a thick piece of grass instead of a thin one?

STUPID GRASS JOKES

Q: What kind of grass sounds more like a banjo than a clarinet?
A: Bluegrass.

Q: What kind of grass pinches your bare feet?
A: Crab grass.

Q: Why do hula dancers wear grass skirts?
A: So you can't see their underwear.

Q: Why is the grass always greener on the other side of the fence?
A: That's where the neighbor's dog likes to pee.

12
SKIP A STONE

"You will find something more in woods than in books. Trees and stones will teach you that which you can never learn from masters."

—Saint Bernard

Cape Cod is a long, hooked peninsula with two completely different kinds of beaches. The ocean side is steep and sandy, with big waves crashing down and licking up against the dunes. But the bay side is shallow and calm, and there are so many smooth, flat rocks you can hardly walk a step without kicking one up from the sand. It's stone-skipping heaven.

One year, as I walked on one of those beaches, I found it—the Holy Grail. The perfect skipping stone. It was jet-black, and perfectly flat on both sides. Its edge was smooth and rounded, and it formed a perfect circle. It was heavy enough to throw for distance, but small enough to fit perfectly into the hollow of my hand.

My brothers wanted me to skip it right away, but there was too much chop in the water and too much crosswind. A stone like that you don't throw under anything but perfect conditions. A stone like that is worth the wait. I slipped it into my pocket and bided my time.

Most of the week, it stayed on the nightstand beside my bed. I toyed with the idea of taking it home, but keeping it in some dark, dusty drawer just didn't seem right. A stone like that had a purpose. It had a destiny.

On the day we were going to leave, I got up early and walked down to the beach. It was low tide and there wasn't a whisper of wind. The calm water stretched all the way out toward the horizon—smooth and unbroken, like a sheet of glass.

I turned the stone in my palm and felt its weight. Then I cradled it between my fingers, took a deep breath, and let it fly.

At first it shot across the water and danced away from me in leaps and bounds. Then, as it slowed, the distance between touches became smaller and smaller until they blended into a single, tapered line. The number of skips was uncountable. They had merged to infinity.

I watched until the last ripples disappeared. Then I turned around and walked back up the beach.

We all have our brushes with eternity—but they come to us only a touch at a time.

WHEN TO START

As soon as kids see someone skip a stone, they're going to want to try it. But unless they already know how to throw a ball or other object, they're going to have a hard time getting the necessary snap in their wrists. On top of that, there's the issue of safety. Stone skipping requires a sidearm motion, and that's hard on little elbows and shoulders.

I'd recommend waiting until your kid is seven or eight, and until she feels comfortable throwing a ball.

WHAT YOU NEED BEFORE YOU START

The requirements are pretty simple: still water and flat stones.

Choppy water makes skipping more difficult. It's not impossible, but for a beginner I'd recommend the smoothest water you can find.

You won't need much of it—even a small swimming pool would do if you didn't mind the collateral damage to the rest of the yard.

As far as stones go, what you need are flat ones. Lots of them. They should be about one to two inches in diameter, and at least four times as wide as they are thick. Ideally, they should be more or less round, and they should have a blunt edge, but neither of these characteristics are crucial.

BASIC TECHNIQUE

Step 1: Grip

Pick out a nice stone and have your child hold it with her throwing hand. Its bottom surface should rest on the bent middle finger, and the thumb should hold it down from the top (see drawing). The index finger should be pressed against the edge of the stone, as shown. If there's a point or an irregularity on the edge that might provide a better grip, that's where the index finger should be touching.

Step 2: Stance

Have your child stand sideways to the water with her feet about a shoulder's width apart. Her elbow should be bent and lifted a bit to the side, with the forearm and hand pointing straight forward (see drawing). The stone should be horizontal to the ground.

Step 3: Spin

This is the hardest thing about skipping, and the least intuitive. When you see people skipping stones, it looks as if they're just throwing rocks at the water as hard as they can. In reality, as much of the motion is designed to create spin as it is to propel the stone forward.

The key to skipping a stone is getting it to stay parallel to the surface of the water. It will do this only if it's spinning rapidly, like a wheel. (For a detailed explanation, see the discussion of gyroscopes in *Chapter 5: Ride a Bike.*) Before we even think about throwing the stone, we have to learn to create that spin.

Have your kid imagine that the stone in her hand is a little wheel, turned sideways so it's parallel to the ground. Using the stance and grip described above, have her flick her wrist forward as if she were spinning the wheel clockwise as fast as she could (see drawing). The index finger provides the force, so it should grip any point or irregularity along the edge of the stone that might give it a better hold.

If your kid is doing the motion correctly, her finger will flick around the edge of the stone and send it spinning. Rather than flying forward, the stone will drop down almost in place, but it will land almost flat. This takes time to master. Keep reminding your child that she isn't throwing the stone yet—she's just spinning it in place like a wheel.

Step 4: Throw

Once your child has mastered the spin, it's time to attempt a throw. Position her in her stance at the edge of the water and have her bend her knees in a slight crouch. The lower she is, the easier it is to keep the stone parallel with the water. She can even tilt her shoulders so her throwing arm drops a little closer to the ground.

Again, tell her to spin the rock, but this time ask her to flick it forward as she snaps her wrist. Have her aim at a spot on the surface about ten feet in front of her. Make sure she keeps her elbow bent and fairly close to the body. And above all, make sure she keeps the stone level and spins it as fast as she can.

At first the rock will just plop into the water. But if she can increase

the speed of the rock while maintaining its spin, there will come a time when a stone skims the surface a little before it sinks. This is cause for lavish praise and encouragement. Swear that you saw a skip. Tell her to keep trying. After that it's just a matter of time.

TROUBLESHOOTING

It can be hard to tell what's wrong when stone after stone just plops into the water and disappears. Here are the most common problems and how to fix them. You may have to just monkey around until you find something that works.

Not Enough Spin

Watch each stone carefully before it hits the water. Is it spinning like a discus or tumbling end over end? If the stone isn't spinning enough, try this trick. Instead of just imagining a wheel, have your kid spin one. Take a toy truck or car and turn it on its side. Have your child grasp one of its wheels as if it's a stone and spin it as hard as she can.

If you can't find a wheel that's big enough, try this. Take an old CD or CD-ROM that you don't need (may I suggest something by the latest teen idol or boy band?), and have your child hold it like a skipping stone over a table or other hard surface. Put a pencil through the hole and press the eraser against the table to hold it in place. Tell her to spin the CD as hard as she can, using her index finger to supply the force. After a few tries, she should have a better idea what it takes to spin a stone.

Not Enough Speed

When you're throwing something big, like a football, you need strength. But in order to throw a small object, you don't need brute force. You need arm speed. When you skip a stone, this is doubly important, because the speed of your hand provides not only forward momentum, but spin.

If your child is throwing her stones in a gentle arc, she needs to generate more velocity. The stone has to hit the surface of the water traveling in almost a straight line. To get this kind of hand speed, she needs to use a motion that works the same way as cracking a whip.

When you crack a whip, you get the thick, heavy part of the whip moving in the right direction, and then you suddenly stop it. The momentum is transferred to the thinner end of the whip which, being much lighter, snaps forward at great speeds. This is what we want to do with your child's arm. (More on the health implications of this later.)

At the start of the motion, the elbow moves forward as the wrist and hand lag behind. When the elbow gets close to the body, it stops, but the hand and forearm continue forward. Finally, the forearm stops, and the wrist snaps forward like the end of a whip. The very tip of the "whip" is the index finger, which gives the stone a final spin as it leaves the hand and ends up pointing forward, where the stone is supposed to go.

This isn't an easy motion to master, but once she gets it, she should have more than enough velocity to skip a stone.

Wrong Throwing Angle

Generally, the more horizontal a throw is, the more likely it is that the stone will skip. If the stone strikes the water too close to the thrower, it comes in at too steep of an angle and it won't bounce. This can be fixed by releasing the stone from a point closer to the ground, but the throw still has to travel out far enough to give the correct angle.

If the stone strikes the water too far from the thrower, other forces come into play. If the throw is weak, it will start to arc downward and lose the proper angle. If it doesn't have enough spin, the stone will begin to tilt in midair.

The perfect distance is the one that gives you the most level stone as it hits the water. This depends on velocity, spin, the quality of the stone, and the height of the stone when it's released. For any given throw, you need to experiment to find the right spot.

Wrong Stone Angle

When the stone hits the water, it should be more or less level. If there's any tilt, it should be with the front edge slightly upward. When the front edge tilts downward, it slices through the surface of the water and there's no skip.

It takes practice to give a stone a slight upward tilt while throwing it at a downward angle. Try turning your hand to tilt the front edge up a little as you grip the stone—a few degrees is enough—and use plenty of spin. If you keep playing around with it, you'll get it.

Bad Rocks

An experienced rock-skipper can skip anything with even a slightly flat surface, but when you're first learning, good stones make a big difference. Generally, bad stones are not flat enough, but occasionally you'll find one that's *too* flat. It's too light for its large surface area, and it tends to flip over in midair—especially if there's a wind. For this problem, you can crouch down low and aim at a spot that's closer. But for stones that aren't flat enough, there's only one solution: find better stones.

SAFETY TIPS

The hazards involved when kids get near water or projectiles are discussed elsewhere in this book, but I should mention one problem that's peculiar to skipping stones. Turning your kid's arm into a whip is a dicey endeavor. I warned against it in the context of sidearm motions in the chapter on throwing a ball. Because skipping stones are light, you can get away with it, but not indefinitely. Once kids learn to skip, they'll want to do it again and again. Don't let them throw every flat stone on the beach. Use common sense and make them stop at the first sign of soreness.

WHY DO STONES SKIP?

No matter how fast you throw a stone, it still strikes the water moving at a downward angle. Why doesn't it just continue down beneath the surface? Why does it skip? The answer is surface tension.

You've seen surface tension at work many times. When a bug walks on water, that's surface tension. When a raindrop stays together instead of breaking apart into mist, that's surface tension. And whenever you blow a bubble, that's surface tension too. But how does it work?

Water molecules are more attracted to each other than they are to the molecules in the air. When water and air meet, as it does at the surface of a pond, the water molecules cling to each other rather than to the air. Because of this, the surface acts like a very thin skin.

When you drop a rock, it breaks the surface tension very easily. But when a spinning stone strikes the water at an almost horizontal angle, the surface tension is strong enough to redirect the stone just slightly, making it skip instead of sink.

Here's a trick you can do to demonstrate surface tension. Take a hair out of your comb or brush and float it on a bowl of water. It is held at the surface by surface tension. Now take a couple of drops of dish soap and drop them near the hair, but not on top of it. The soap molecules get between the water molecules and keep them from holding onto each other. The surface tension breaks, and the hair sinks.

This is why soap cleans things. It helps water molecules let go of each other so they can penetrate the dirt and grease and dissolve it.

ANYONE CARE FOR A SKIFF?

In Ireland skipping stones is called "skiffing." In Denmark it's known as "smutting." The Swedish call it "smorgas," and the British call it "ducks and drakes."

Even in America, serious stone-skippers have a language all their own. When they skip a stone, the resulting series of skips is called a "run." Each hop, when it's cleanly separated from the ones before and after, is a "plink." At the end of the run there may be a series of short hops that run together. These are called "pitty-pats."

Of course, not every run is all plinks and pitty-pats. When a stone just sinks without a single hop, it's called a "plonk." And worst of all, there's the stone that never even hits the water. That, in the world of serious skipping, is a "skronker."

WORLD RECORD SKIPPIN'

In 1994, Jerdone McGhee skipped a run of thirty-eight plinks on the Blanco River.

EVER SKIP A ROCKET SHIP?

Let's hope not. A lot of scientists have worked very hard to keep this from happening. It turns out that the Earth's atmosphere has a sort of surface tension where it meets the vacuum of outer space. When a spaceship like the Space Shuttle reenters the atmosphere, it has to pick its angle very carefully. If it comes in too steep, it will generate too much friction and heat and burn up. But if it comes in too shallow, it will deflect off the atmosphere like a stone on a pond and skip into outer space, never to be seen again.

ROCK-ROCK JOKES

Q: What did the stone say when the rock forgot to call?
A: "I think you're taking me for granite."

Q: What were the talking stone's last words?
A: "Oh, just skip it!"

               *   *   *

Teacher: I'd like you to write an essay on sedimentary rock.
Student: Okay, but my notebook's going to get awful heavy.

13
MAKE A PAPER AIRPLANE

"When the flight is not high the fall is not heavy."
—Chinese proverb

When we were in third grade, my friend George Markowitz and I used to play a game called the "Land of Death." This is how it worked.

We'd push the couch in George's living room up against the wall and put all our small plastic animals and soldiers on top of it. This was the "Doomed Planet." On the other side of the room was the armchair. That was the "Safe Planet." In between was a vast stretch of floor that we'd fill with pillow mountain ranges, Saran Wrap rivers, and every flesh-eating plastic dinosaur, predatory mammal, and deadly obstacle that two nine-year-old boys could devise. This, of course, was the "Land of Death."

Using big pieces of poster paper, we'd make giant paper airplanes to transport the tiny figures on the Doomed Planet to the Safe Planet across the room. Of course, many a transport ship veered tragically off course and crash-landed in the Land of Death. This led to an afternoon of grisly dinosaur attacks, quicksand fatalities, and heroic rescue parties. Sometimes George's cat would play, adding a note of reality to the maimings and making the game better still.

One day, George decided it would be a great idea to add some special effects to the crash of one transport ship. He stole his mother's cigarette lighter and sent the big paper plane soaring across the room with its tail engulfed in flames. The effect was quite stunning, but we didn't have much time to enjoy it. It landed on a pillow, which immediately started to burn.

It was the only time in my life I did something that stupid and got away with it. We put out the fire without triggering any smoke alarms, and we buried the pillow in George's backyard. As far as I know, his mother never noticed it was missing, or at least she never said anything if she did.

After that we moved the "Land of Death" outdoors. We never tried to reproduce that pyrotechnic landing, but we remembered it often, with a strange mixture of fondness and fear.

WHEN TO START

There are thousands of paper airplane designs out there, and more of them are showing up all the time. Many are simple, but some require an origami tour de force.

For this chapter, I've chosen the two easiest models I know. Any kid with a little manual dexterity and some patience should be able to handle them. For most kids, this is about age five or six.

WHAT YOU NEED BEFORE YOU START

The ideal paper for folding airplanes is fairly lightweight, but stiff enough to hold a crease and keep its shape in flight. Luckily, that describes the all-purpose paper you'll find in almost any printer or copy machine. Start with a fresh supply of crisp, clean sheets—enough so you can experiment without fear of running out.

The only other things you'll need are a firm, flat surface for folding and a big room or a windless day for flying.

BASIC TECHNIQUE: FOLDING

Folding Fundamentals

A little bit of care goes a long way when you're folding airplanes. Straight, precise folds with sharp creases make for an airworthy plane. The models below are more forgiving than most, but the more carefully they're made, the better they'll fly.

The Jet

This classic design is the one most kids learn first. It's fast, and it throws well for distance. When folding it, try to keep both sides as symmetric as possible, and make the creases nice and sharp near the narrow nose of the plane.

Step 1

Fold an 8½ by 11 sheet of paper lengthwise, creasing it right down the middle. From now on I'll refer to this folded edge as the "center crease."

Step 2

Take one of the free corners and fold it down, so that the short edge lines up with the center crease, creating a 45-degree angle at the nose of the plane. Turn the plane over and fold down the same corner on the other side.

Step 3

Take the new edge and fold it down to the center crease once again. This cuts the 45-degree angle in half, further narrowing the nose. Turn the plane over and repeat on the other side.

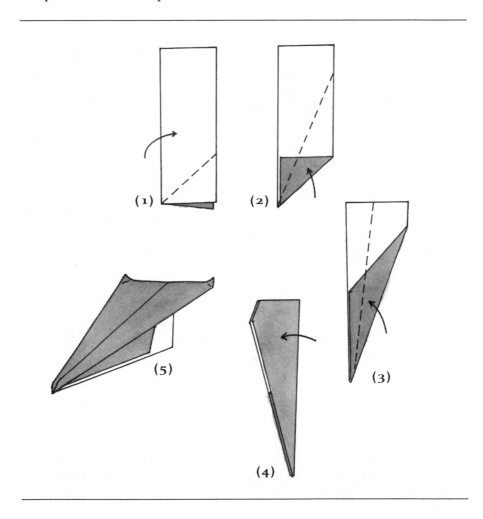

Step 4

Once again, fold the new edge down to the center crease. Now the nose is very narrow, so fold carefully to make sure the new crease goes all the way out to the tip.

Step 5

Finally, unfold this last fold just enough to spread the wings.

Notice how sharp that tip is. If that makes you nervous, undo Step 4 and open up the center crease. Fold back the last inch to inch and a half of the tip, then refold the center crease and repeat Step 4. This will give you a blunt tip that cuts down on eye-poking potential without affecting performance.

The Glider

This design is simplicity itself. Part of the fun is that it doesn't really look like it should fly. It doesn't go very fast, but it has a lot of hang time, making it a good choice for graceful glides from second-story windows.

Step 1

Fold an $8\frac{1}{2}$ by 11 sheet of paper widthwise to establish a center crease. Then unfold it and flip it over, so the ridge of the crease points up.

Step 2

Fold one of the long edges to create a flap that's an inch wide along its entire length. Press down the crease to make it as thin as possible.

Step 3

Fold the flap over four more times, pressing down with each fold to make sure it stays as thin as possible. Now, the width of the flap is still about an inch, but the total width of the paper, including the flap, is only $3\frac{1}{2}$ inches, or a little less.

Step 4

Fold the sheet in half, along the center crease that you made in Step 1. The flap should be on the outside.

Step 5

One inch from the center crease and parallel to it, make another fold on each side to create the wings. Unfold the wings partway, so the wings make a Y-shape when you grasp the center crease.

BASIC TECHNIQUE: FLYING

Be Prepared to Fiddle

Only rarely will a plane perform perfectly on its maiden flight. Very small differences in symmetry, folding technique, and paper thickness have a big impact on aerodynamics. You should expect to make adjustments to get each plane to fly, and then keep making them as the

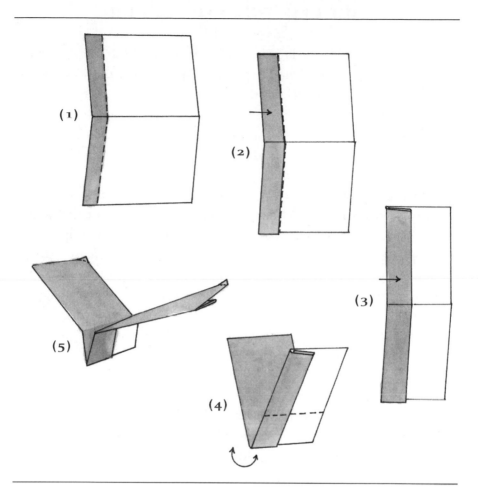

wear and tear of launches and landings leave their inevitable dents and bends.

The Launch

How you throw a plane has a big impact on how it flies. However, since every plane is different, I can't give you precise instructions. You'll just have to mess around and see what works.

The first variable in a launch is where you hold the plane. A good place to begin is at the balance point, or a little in front of it. Some planes, though, are best held at the very front, and a few are launched from the back.

The second thing to mess around with is the launch angle. For starters, try a level launch, but don't be afraid to angle up or down to adjust for an individual plane's idiosyncrasies.

The last thing to consider is the force of the launch, also known as the thrust. Fast, streamlined planes like the Jet can be launched with a lot of speed. Slower planes, like the Glider, require a gentler approach. Every plane performs differently at different speeds. Again, experimentation is the key.

Kids often try to throw a paper airplane as if it were a baseball. Get them to use a quick flick of the wrist instead. The amount of force will be better controlled, and the launch angle will be more consistent.

TROUBLESHOOTING

If just messing around with your launch doesn't do the trick, you can always take a more analytical approach. Here are the different kinds of flight instability and some ways to address them.

Diving

If your plane goes nose down, even at different launch speeds and angles, try bending up the back corners of the plane. As the air rushes over the wings, it will push against these upturned corners and keep the tail of the plane down.

Stalling

A stall is when the nose of the plane tilts upward and the plane loses all of its forward momentum. Again, launch speed and angle play a big role here. But if those adjustments don't work, try bending the tail corners down.

Another approach is to add some weight to the front of the plane. The easiest way to do this is to slip a paper clip over the central crease, somewhere near the tip. Notice that this pinches the crease together and changes the angle of the wings, so you may have to readjust those folds.

Rolling

When a plane rolls over in midair, it often means that the wings are angled downward. Most planes fly best when the wings are level, or tilted slightly up. The tricky part is that wings may *seem* level when you hold the plane to launch it but tilt downward during flight when the center crease comes apart. Adjust the wings so they're level when the plane is *in the air.*

Veering

When a plane keeps turning to one side, it isn't necessarily a bad thing. Throwing planes around the corner into a room full of unsuspecting people is a lot of fun. But if you want the plane to fly straight, here are a few tips.

Check the symmetry of the plane. Asymmetric folding usually results in asymmetric flights. Also, check the symmetry of the wing angles, and adjust as needed.

In most planes, the central crease acts like a keel to keep the plane from veering off course. However, in models like the Glider, which don't have much of a keel, you may need to add more vertical edges to keep it flying straight. Try folding the outer edge of the wings up or down, making sure they remain parallel to the direction of flight.

AMAZING PAPER PLANE FACTS

The largest flyable paper airplane was built by a group of university students in Holland. It had a wingspan of more than 45 feet, and it flew a distance of 114 feet from an elevated platform.

The record for longest throw by distance belongs to Tony Felch of the United States. He threw a paper airplane 193 feet, indoors on level ground. The longest throw by time aloft belongs to Ken Blackburn, also of the United States. His plane stayed in the air 27.6 seconds!

For the sake of comparison, the Wright brothers' first flight covered only 120 feet and stayed aloft for 12 seconds.

HOW TO STEER AN AIRPLANE

Real airplanes aren't all that different from paper ones. The same forces keep both of them on course and in the air. The next time you see a big jetliner, take a look at all the moving parts on the wings and tail.

On the trailing edge of the wings are three sets of movable panels. The ones nearest the passenger compartment are called flaps and spoilers. The flaps tilt down and create additional lift during takeoffs and landings. The spoilers tilt up after touchdown, to counteract the lift of the wings and to slow the plane down.

The outer panels move in opposite directions—when one side goes up, the other goes down. These are called ailerons, and they stop a plane from rolling to one side or the other. In stunt planes they can be used to *create* a roll. Try bending the back corners of a paper plane in opposite directions—one up and one down. Voilà! Instant stunt plane.

At the back of the plane are a pair of small wings on either side of the tail, called horizontal stabilizers. These have panels along their back edge, called elevators. As they move up or down, they cause the plane to go higher or lower, just like you do when you bend the corners at the back of a paper airplane.

Finally, the upright fin of the tail, the vertical stabilizer, has a flap that moves to the left or right, causing the plane to turn. This is the rudder, and you can reproduce it by cutting flaps at the back of a paper plane's keel on either side of the central crease. Bend out the left flap and the plane veers left. Bend out the right flap and it turns right.

PAPER AIRPLANE OLYMPICS

Assuming you aren't going to introduce your kids to the "Land of Death," there are still some cool things you can do with paper airplanes. Around our house, a big favorite is the Paper Airplane Olympics.

Fold a whole bunch of paper planes, using different designs, sizes, and types of paper. Decorate them to give them individual personalities—you can name them if you like. Then let the games begin.

Distance, hang time, accuracy, curved flight, stunts, and almost anything else you can think of can serve as the basis for an event. Let the planes compete head-to-head, using elimination rounds if necessary. Award individual and team medals. Hum their national anthems. It's a great time, especially on a rainy day when everyone has cabin fever.

STUPID FLYING JOKES

Q: Who failed to invent the airplane?
A: The Wrong brothers!

*　　*　　*

One year, little Willie and his sister Velma went to the county fair. Their mother had given them five dollars each that they could spend any way they wanted.

Every time Willie wanted to buy something, Velma stopped him.

"Don't buy that," she'd say. "That ain't worth no five dollars. Don't you know anything? Five dollars is a lot of money!"

Eventually, Willie spotted something at the back of the fairgrounds. It was a shiny red stunt plane! He ran off to have a closer look, ignoring Velma, who yelled at him to stay put then ran after him.

A sign above the plane read: $10 FOR THE RIDE OF YOUR LIFE!

"That sounds like a good deal," said Willie.

"Don't be stupid!" said Velma. "That boring old ride ain't worth no ten dollars! When you gonna get it into your thick head that ten dollars is a lot of money?"

"Is that so?" said the pilot, who had been standing nearby, listening. "I'll have you know that this here plane ride is the most exciting thing you'll ever do, young lady. And what's more, I'll prove it. I'll take the two of you up right this minute. If you can both stay quiet for the whole ride, I'll give ten dollars to *you*. But if I hear one peep out of you—one whoop, or scream, or even a word—then you have to give ten dollars to me. But of course, I understand if you're scared—"

"I ain't scared!" said Velma. She dragged little Willie up into the open, rear cockpit, and off they went.

That pilot did every last trick he knew. He tried barrel rolls, nose-dives, and loop-de-loops. But no matter what he did, the kids didn't say a thing.

Finally, when he ran out of tricks, he landed the plane. As it rolled to a stop, he took ten dollars out of his pocket and turned around.

"I've got to hand it to you," he said. "I never thought you'd make it."

"Me neither," said Willie. "I almost said something when Velma fell out—but ten dollars is a lot of money."

*   *   *

A newspaper photographer was assigned to cover a huge hurricane that was sweeping up the coast. After hours of phone calls, he finally located a pilot who was crazy enough to take him up and fly him right into the eye of the storm.

When he arrived at the local airstrip, he saw a tiny plane sitting on the tarmac.

"Let's go," he said as he jumped into the cockpit. They taxied down the runway and took off. "Head south," he ordered. "Just follow the coast, and don't change course unless I tell you to."

A half an hour later they approached the storm front. It looked like a black wall of death, reaching from the angry sea all the way up to the heavens. Lightning flashed all around them and the plane shook and veered crazily in the wind. The photographer pulled out his camera and began taking pictures.

"What in the world are you doing?" asked the pilot.

"What does it look like? I'm taking photos. That's what photographers get paid to do."

"Photographer?" said the pilot. "You mean, you aren't the flight instructor?"

14
DO A MAGIC TRICK

"Nothing I do can't be done by a ten-year-old . . . with fifteen years of practice."

—*magician Harry Blackstone Jr.*

One summer, when I was about ten, we went to New York for a relative's wedding, and I ended up riding to the banquet with my cousin Douglas. Doug liked fancy cars and pretty girls, and his business dealings were a little shady. He was our favorite cousin. He taught us kung fu moves when our parents weren't looking, and we always had a crush on his latest girlfriend.

As we walked from his car to the restaurant, Doug took me on a shortcut down a dark, dingy street, and we passed an old man lying on the sidewalk. He smelled of urine and beer.

"Hey, little man," he croaked, pointing a shaky finger at me. "Give me a quarter—I'll show you a trick."

I jumped back and grabbed Doug's arm.

"What are you scared of?" said Doug. "He's just a wino." He pulled a quarter out of his pocket and tossed it in the air.

The old man caught it and held it out for me to see. Then, with one quick motion, he made it vanish into thin air.

"Come here," he said. He was missing most of his front teeth. I glanced nervously at Doug. He nodded. When I stepped forward, the old man reached behind my ear. Suddenly, the coin was back in his hand.

"Do it again," I said.

He did the trick for me three more times.

"Come on," said Doug. "We have to go."

"Much obliged," said the old man. "Much obliged."

As we walked away, I looked back at him. He flashed his toothless grin and waved.

In the restaurant, I wanted to tell everyone what had happened, but I hesitated. My parents never would have let me talk to a wino on the street. I kept the story to myself. Later on, I asked Doug if he knew how to make money disappear too.

"Oh, yeah," he said. "It disappears so fast, even I don't know where it goes."

WHEN TO START

Coin tricks require a certain amount of dexterity. I've chosen the two easiest ones I know, but you still might wait until your child is eight or nine.

WHAT YOU NEED BEFORE YOU START

These tricks will work with many small objects, but I like coins because they're easy to find and uniform in shape and size. For most kids, a quarter is a good size, but adults will have an easier time with a half-dollar. The only other thing you'll need is a good-sized mirror.

BASIC TECHNIQUE

The key to making a small object disappear is to make the audience believe that it's somewhere it's not. This is usually accomplished by pretending to move the object from one hand to the other (a pass), and then hiding the coin in the first hand (a palm). The rest is just showmanship and misdirection.

Usually I recommend learning a skill at the same time as your kid, but this one is fun to learn first, on your own. After you do it for him a couple of times, he'll be begging you to show him how.

The Thumb Palm

This is the easiest palm to learn, but it has some drawbacks. The coin is hidden from the audience only when the hand is in certain positions, and it takes practice to maintain those positions while keeping the hand relaxed and natural. Let's start with the mechanics of the palm maneuver, then incorporate the pass and the misdirection.

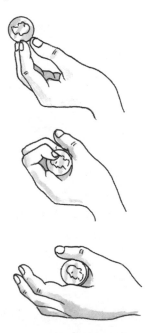

Step 1: The palm

Start by holding the coin between the tips of the index and middle fingers. Bring the tip of your thumb up to the edge of the coin to make the grip seem more natural. Show as much of the coin as possible, so its disappearance will be more impressive.

Now, move the thumb out of the way a little, and bend the index and middle fingers so they deposit the coin in the crotch between the base of the thumb and the palm. The coin should be held gently by its edges. Extend the index and middle fingers to a natural, relaxed position, but leave the tips of the thumb and index finger close together. Now, when viewed from the palm side, the hand appears to be empty. The thumb completely hides the coin.

Practice palming the coin and then extracting it with the same two fingers. When both maneuvers are quick, reliable, and completely natural, move on to the next step.

Step 2: The pass

The key to any pass is to duplicate exactly the movements you would use to actually transfer the coin from one hand to the other. The best way to do this is to practice in front of a mirror.

Stand in front of a mirror that's big enough so you can see yourself from your head to your knees. Hold up the coin at chest level, using your thumb and two fingers just as before. With a smooth, unhurried motion, wrap your other hand around the coin with its palm facing toward you. Take the coin in your fist and extend it toward the audience, letting the first hand fall slowly and casually to your side. Do this several times, paying close attention to how each hand moves. Notice that a fist with a coin in it looks different than a tightly closed, empty fist.

Now, using the exact same motion, bring your hand up to wrap around the coin, but instead of transferring it, palm it. Make a fist as if the coin has changed hands, and extend it to the audience just as before. Let the hand with the palmed coin fall slowly to your side, keeping the palm facing the audience so the thumb hides the coin. The hand position will look more natural if your body is turned a little toward the palming side.

Practice the pass in front of the mirror until it looks exactly the same as an actual transfer of the coin.

Step 3: The trick

Now that you can dazzle them with dexterity, you have to learn to baffle them with bull crap. The aim is to distract the audience from what you're really doing by any means possible. This is harder for kids than adults, because they aren't as practiced at casual deception. Believe me, though, they take to it with great glee when given the opportunity.

First, distract them with timing. Make the pass as nonchalantly as possible, when the audience thinks the trick hasn't even begun. After the coin is safely palmed, have a member of the audience blow on your empty fist or tap it with a magic wand to make the coin disappear. Be creative—a little showmanship can go a long way.

Second, distract the audience with movement. The palming hand stays quiet and inanimate. It holds the coin very still, for all the audience to see. Let the other hand gesture and move as you talk. Then, after the active hand supposedly takes the coin, make sure it moves toward the audience and keeps on moving. The palming hand then falls slowly and gently to your side, where no one will pay it any attention. Practice this in front of the mirror, making sure the palming hand stays as relaxed and natural as possible.

Finally, distract the audience with your eyes. If your gaze follows the empty fist, so will your audience's. This is a subtle point, but it makes a huge difference, and it's well worth practicing.

Once the empty fist is opened and the coin has "disappeared," there are a couple of ways to make it reappear. One is to hold your hands out to either side with palms forward to demonstrate that they are "empty," and then clap them together, producing the coin between the palms. The other is to reach behind an audience member's ear and quickly reverse the palming maneuver. If you push the rim of the coin up with your thumb, you can squeeze it between your thumb and index finger, making it look as if you plucked it out of thin air.

The French Drop and Finger Palm

This method is a little harder to learn, but it makes for a better illusion. If done properly, the pass makes the audience believe they've seen the transfer with their own eyes, and the palm keeps the hand in a very natural position.

Step 1: The drop

Start by holding the coin by its edges between the thumb and index fingers. This time, unlike with the thumb palm, you'll want to hold it with your weak hand.

Hold your hand in front of you so its back is to the audience, but cup it slightly, and let the ring and little fingers bend a bit more than the others. Now, with as little movement as possible, let go of the coin and let it drop. With a little adjustment of hand and finger position, you should be able to drop the coin so it ends up in the little funnel created by your fingers.

Now, practice the actual transfer in front of the mirror, just as you did with the thumb palm. Hold the coin in front of you, and use the other hand to snatch it away, with the thumb passing under the

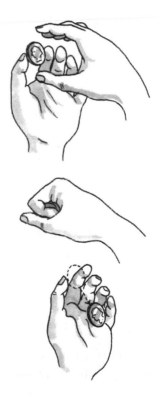

coin and the fingers curling over the top. The first hand holds the coin still while the snatching hand grabs the coin and continues moving toward the audience. The empty holding hand then falls slowly to your side.

To make the pass, go to snatch the coin as you did before, but drop the coin just as the fingers curl around it. The coin ends up cradled in the holding hand, and the snatching hand is now an empty fist. If you practice this in front of the mirror, it looks as if you can actually see the snatching hand take the coin. It helps if the audience views the coin edgewise, so they don't see it flash as it drops.

Step 2: The palm

In this case, the palm is continuous with the drop. By positioning the hand and fingers just so, you can get the coin to lodge between the bent fingers and the crease between the base of the fingers and the palm. This is by far the hardest part of the trick. Keep experimenting with the hand and the coin at different angles, and with the fingers bent to different degrees. Ideally, the coin will be secured by the ring and little fingers, which look the most natural when they're bent, but the middle finger works too.

You may need to bend the fingers slightly to "catch" the coin as it drops, but make the motion as subtle as possible. After that, let the palming hand fall slowly to the side, with the palm turned away from the audience.

Step 3: The trick

There's nothing much new here. Everything that applies to the thumb palm also applies to the French drop. Use your timing, your movement, and your gaze to misdirect the audience. Make the palming hand as relaxed and natural as possible, and make your empty fist look like it's holding something.

TROUBLESHOOTING

Dropped Coins

This is mainly a problem with the French drop. Try experimenting with the tilt of the coin before it's dropped. Monkey around with the finger and hand position. If all else fails, try a larger coin.

Mannequin Hands

A stiff, unnatural palming hand is a dead giveaway. Most of the time, you can fix the problem with some practice in front of the mirror. Try holding the coin with a lighter grip. Remember to spread the fingers slightly. Again, a change in coin size might do the trick.

Flashing Coins

With the thumb palm, this is a problem of hand position. Remember to bring the tips of the thumb and index finger close together, and always keep the palm of the hand toward the audience. On the French drop, make sure the coin is edgewise to the audience as it drops, and try to curl the fingers of the snatching hand over the coin before you let go of it. As always, practicing in front of a mirror will correct most problems.

THE GREATEST MAGICIAN YOU NEVER HEARD OF

These days, the big magic shows that you see in Las Vegas or on TV all use elaborate sets and equipment to create their illusions. Even the great Houdini rigged special crates and trunks to help him make his amazing escapes. But around the late 1800s, one of the most famous magicians in the world used no special props or equipment to create his act. All he needed was a stack of coins and a deck of cards.

T. Nelson Downs was the undisputed father of modern sleight-of-hand. He invented a number of coin and card manipulations, many of which are still required study for every magician learning his craft. The thumb palm described above is just a variation on what has come to be known as "Downs's Palm." Using that palm, he was able to conceal twenty half-dollars at once in a single hand, producing them at his fingertips one at a time. He developed that skill at the age of fifteen.

ACCESSORY MUSCLES

The more advanced sleight-of-hand tricks depend on the magician's ability to manipulate his or her fingers in ways that wouldn't seem possible. Magicians do this by training and strengthening the accessory muscles in their hands.

Most of the time, when we grab or hold an object, we use the muscles of our forearm. These muscles are fairly large and strong. Try this: hold up one hand with the palm facing toward you and your fingers relaxed and partly curled. Now, use your other hand to squeeze the middle of your forearm, pressing your thumb briskly into the muscles at the front of the arm.

You'll notice that your middle, ring, and little fingers all curl. That's because these muscles attach to a single tendon, which then spreads out and attaches to each finger, allowing them to move as one.

The forearm muscles aren't the only ones that control our fingers. There are small muscles in the fingers and hand that we seldom use. By training these, a magician—or a pianist or flutist—can learn to move the fingers independently.

You can use these muscles too, if you learn to control them. Try bending your ring finger toward your palm as quickly as you can. Most likely, the middle finger and the little finger bent too. That's because you used the big muscles of your forearm. Now try to bend the ring finger very slowly, without moving the other fingers. This time, the other fingers don't follow nearly as much. With enough practice, you could learn to move just your ring finger while the others stayed straight and still.

STUPID MAGICIAN JOKES

Q: Why do magicians make good soccer players?
A: Because they make so many hat tricks!

Q: What did one magician say to the other?
A: "Hey, who was that woman I sawed you with last night?"

Q: Why do magicians always tip their hats at the end of the show?
A: To get out the rabbit poop.

15
EAT WITH CHOPSTICKS

"Never eat anything at one sitting that you can't lift."
—Miss Piggy

In my family, the ability to use chopsticks was not optional—it was a matter of survival. All of our meals were served "family style." This meant that a platter of food was tossed into the middle of the table, and my brothers and I would lunge and grab until all of it was gone.

Of course, chopsticks had other uses as well. They made great drumsticks when we played along with our Beatles albums. They formed the girders and beams for countless miniature construction projects in our backyard. And at Chinese wedding banquets, while the drunken uncles droned on in a language we didn't understand, we used them to impale roasted chicken heads and chase each other around the tables.

I suppose the ability to use chopsticks doesn't qualify as an important life skill, but you never know when it might come in handy. When my wife and I were first dating, I took her out to dim sum. Not only did she gulp down the spicy beef tendon without a blink, but she managed to lift the slimy little morsels with her chopsticks. I knew, right then and there, I'd met the woman of my dreams.

WHEN TO START

Kids love to do anything that involves playing with their food, and using chopsticks (especially for beginners) is practically food hockey. Still, to use chopsticks well, you need some hand strength and some fine motor skills. Every kid acquires these in his own time, but with practice, most will be successful by about age six.

WHAT YOU NEED BEFORE YOU START

There are all kinds of chopsticks out there. The Japanese use ones made of lacquered wood that taper to a point. These require a bit too much dexterity for some beginners. Many Chinese restaurants use plastic ones that work just fine, though they can be a little slippery.

Surprisingly, the best ones for teaching kids are the disposable wooden ones that you have to break apart before you use them. They're a little lighter and shorter than most, and they have a good grip. Hold them by the free ends and pull gently until they separate, then rub them together to remove any splinters.

If you buy your own, I'd recommend bamboo. They're light and sturdy, and they give you an excellent grip.

BASIC TECHNIQUE

The first thing you need to know is that, when in use, the two chopsticks have very different roles. The bottom stick is rock solid. It stays still while the upper stick pivots to pinch down against it. The two sticks touch only at the very tip.

Most instructions for using chopsticks—including the ones on the little paper sleeve they come in at restaurants—tell you to hold the moving chopstick as if it were a pencil. This is a mistake. The pencil grip is meant to produce the tiny, precise movements we use to write. What we want for picking up food is something stronger and more stable. This is especially important for kids, because their finger strength is much less than that of adults.

Step 1

Since the pencil grip is familiar to everyone, we'll start there and alter it. Have your kid grip one chopstick about two inches from its tip, as if he were going to write with it. Notice that it rests on top of the middle finger. Without moving the thumb and index finger, have him move the middle finger so that its tip rests against the side of the chopstick right beside the index finger.

Now the stick is squeezed between the side of the index finger and tip of the middle finger on one side, and the thumb on the other. Bending and straightening the middle and index fingers should move the tip of the stick up and down without any loss of grip.

Step 2

Leaving this first stick in place, slide the other one below it so it rests in the notch between the hand and the base of the thumb. This bottom stick is held firmly in place by the tip of the ring finger and the hand on one side, and the base of the thumb on the other. Make sure the tips of the two sticks are even, and that, when parallel, they are separated as much as possible (by at least half an inch).

Step 3

Now, using the index and middle fingers to supply the force, have your child pinch the tip of the upper stick down onto the lower one. If

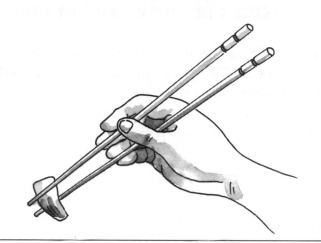

the tips miss each other, adjust the upper stick by changing the pressure applied to the side of the stick by the middle finger.

Once the tips are pinching together, it's time to pick up something. A crumpled piece of napkin or tissue paper is a good start. From there, it's a quick jump to won-ton and snow peas!

TROUBLESHOOTING

Weak Grip

The most common problem is the inability to grip the food with enough force. Check the position of the upper stick and make sure the middle and index fingers are both working to push its tip downward. If that doesn't work, try moving the hand closer to the tip of the sticks. (See below to find out why this makes the grip stronger.)

Pickup Sticks

If the sticks keep clattering on the table, take a close look at the way they're held. Both sticks get their stability from three points of contact:

the thumb on the middle of one side pushing against the tip of a finger and the side of the palm or index finger on the other. Dropped sticks usually mean that one of these points isn't secure.

The most likely culprit is the ring finger against the bottom stick. To shore up this point, have your kid put the tips of his ring and pinky fingers together and nestle the stick into the crease between them.

Tough Grips

Some things are just plain difficult to pick up with chopsticks. If it's heavy, or slippery, or both, you might want to use a spoon or a fork. Don't worry, there's no shame in that. After all, there are spoons in China too.

On the other end of the tough pickup spectrum is rice. Many a native chopstick user has stared in disbelief while someone at the next table chased his rice around his plate a grain at a time. If you want to look like a pro, here's what you should do.

When the food comes, ask for a rice bowl and fill it about two-thirds full with rice. You can mix in some meat or vegetables and a little sauce if you like. Now, cupping the bottom of the bowl in your nonchopstick hand, lift the rim to your mouth and use your chopsticks to scoop in the rice.

At first you'll feel a little self-conscious, but that's the price of being au courant. After all, when in Shanghai . . .

DIM SUM

Now that you've got a family full of chopstick masters, it's time to use your newfound skills for their highest calling: dim sum!

Dim sum, which means "a touch of heart," is a Chinese meal that consists of tiny, carefully prepared dishes of many kinds. There are dumplings, meats, noodles, and sweets in seemingly endless variety. Many Chinese restaurants serve dim sum, especially on weekends, and it's a great adventure for the whole family. It's the perfect chance to show off your chopstick chops.

When you go to dim sum, don't expect a menu. Servers will be circulating around the restaurant with metal carts full of food. They'll lift the lids off little steamers and let you pick what you want. Don't be surprised if they can't explain what each dish contains. Just point at anything that looks good, and if you discover that it's chicken feet, go on to something else.

At some restaurants, they add up the tab by counting the serving plates on the table. Unless you read Chinese, your check will be unintelligible, but don't worry. Most of the time the bill is surprisingly small.

CHOPSTICK FACTS

Origins

Chopsticks have been the eating utensil of choice for centuries in most of East Asia, including Japan, Korea, China, and Vietnam. They probably originated in China, where they're called *k'uai-tzu,* meaning "something fast." English-speaking traders mispronounced the word as *chop,* which is how chopsticks eventually got their name.

What About That Annoying Song?

The piano piece "Chopsticks" has nothing to do with Chinese food. It was a novelty piece, written by a sixteen-year-old girl named Euphonia Allen in 1877, and published under the pen name "Arthur de Lulli." In the sheet music, the pianist was instructed to turn the hands sideways and play the notes with a chopping motion, thus giving the piece its name.

Department of Dubious Distinctions

A British man named Dean Gould once ate fifty-one individual grains of rice with chopsticks in just three minutes. Someone give that man a rice bowl.

Chopstick Etiquette

Chopsticks figure prominently in some parts of the Buddhist funeral rites in Japan. For this reason, to handle them in certain ways can unintentionally invoke an association with death.

For example, it's bad luck in Japan to leave one's chopsticks standing upright in a bowl, because that's the way they're positioned in offerings to the deceased. It's also frowned upon to pass food to someone else using your chopsticks. This is how fragments of a cremated body are lifted from the funeral pyre and passed among the mourners. Try not to think about that when you're eating, though.

CHOPSTICK PHYSICS

Back in the chapter on throwing a ball, we talked about levers. We showed how the end of a longer lever arm travels farther and at greater speeds. But that speed comes at a price. We can illustrate what is lost with a round of Chopstick Wrestling.

Place two chopsticks at right angles, overlapping them by about an inch at the tips. Bind the tips together with a rubber band. You and your child should sit across from one another with your elbows on a table, as if you were going to arm wrestle.

With the backs of your hands facing one another, each of you should grasp one of the chopsticks as if it were the upper stick in your normal eating grip. To start with, each of you should hold your stick as far from the crossed tips as possible.

Using only your fingers and wrists, each of you tries to force the tip of the other person's chopstick toward you. Most likely, you'll be stronger than your child. Now, have him slide his hand along his chopstick until it's just an inch or so from the crossed tips. You should leave your hand where it is. Try another round. This time he'll defeat you easily.

When you hold a pair of chopsticks near the tip, you shorten the lever arm. This lets you pinch down with more force and enables you to pick up bigger and slimier things. How's *that* for motivation?

THE JEDI CHOPSTICK MASTER

After working up a big appetite doing battle with the Imperial Empire, Luke Skywalker decided to treat himself to dinner at a Chinese restaurant. When his food arrived, he picked up a pair of chopsticks and tried to put some noodles on his plate. They slipped out and slopped all over the table. Then he tried to pick up a dumpling, but it ended up in his drink. Again and again he tried to use the chopsticks, but he dropped every last bit of food before it reached his mouth. Finally, in frustration and disgust, he hurled the chopsticks to the floor.

Just then he heard the voice of his slain teacher, Obi-Wan Kenobi.

"Luke . . . Luke . . ." said the disembodied voice.

"Yes," said Luke. "I hear you, Obi-Wan. Please help and guide me, as you have always done before."

"Luke . . ." said the voice, "use the forks."

16
BUILD A WOODEN BOX

> *"To do good work, one must first have good tools."*
> —*Chinese proverb*

In sixth grade I took a woodworking class. It lasted only a few weeks, and we were supposed to design and complete one project for our final grade. I decided to make a footstool for my mom.

I remember how carefully I cut the pieces and chiseled out the joints. I found a leftover scrap from our carpet at home, and I used it to cover the top of the stool. When I brought it home, my mom made a big fuss over it. She especially liked the way it matched the carpet in our house. I practically swelled with pride.

As the years passed, my pride diminished. In truth, the stool was pretty ugly. The joints were ragged, the finish was uneven, and the carpet on top began to unravel at the corners. After a while I was almost embarrassed that I'd built it. I asked my mom why she kept it around. Why didn't she buy a *real* stool?

"What for?" she said. "It works fine. Why should I waste money on a new one?"

That was a common refrain in my house. My parents are thrifty people—they never spend money on things they don't need. I knew there was no use arguing. The stool would stay until it fell apart.

Last year I went to visit my folks in their new town house. I was amazed to see the ugly footstool sitting in the middle of their living room. It looked the same as always, only a little more ragged. It didn't even match the carpet anymore.

"I can't believe you held on to that ugly stool," I said.

"It's not so ugly," said my mom. "Besides, you made it for me."

I finally realized that thrift wasn't the only reason she kept it. I guess footstools are like people. There are some that only a mother could love.

WHEN TO START

Working with hand tools takes a certain amount of strength and coordination. It also requires enough maturity to treat the tools with respect, and not as toys. Usually, these things don't come together until about age eight at the earliest, and for many kids not until around age ten.

WHAT YOU NEED BEFORE YOU START

I've tried to make this project as simple as possible, to cut down on the hassle and expense. Still, if you have no tools at all, you'll end up spending a little money. Consider it an investment. A good tool can last a lifetime, if cared for properly, and after a while it can start to feel like an old friend.

Draw up a list of what you need and take a trip to the local hardware store. Make sure you bring your kid, and leave enough time to look around. The array of tools and building materials is a great inspiration for any aspiring carpenter.

Tools

- *Claw hammer.* This is a standard hammer with the V-shaped claw on the back for pulling out nails. Small ones are available, but a kid can also use a standard size and choke up on the handle.
- *Handsaw.* The best choice is probably a crosscut saw. These are designed to cut across wood grain, and their teeth are smaller, which makes them easier to handle. You could also buy an all-purpose saw that cuts both across and with the grain. It's more versatile, but the longer teeth make it harder to use at the start of a cut. As with hammers, small sizes are available, but most kids can handle a normal, adult size.
- *Tape measure or ruler.*
- *Carpenter's square (optional).* This is an L-shaped metal tool for making right angles. It's nice to have, but you can also use something else with a perfect 90-degree angle, like the end of a board, or even this book.
- *Sandpaper.* Aluminum oxide paper is the least expensive. Get a couple of sheets each of a coarse paper (around 60 grit) and a fine one (150 grit).
- *Saftey glasses.* One pair for each of you.

Materials and Supplies

- *Wood.* For this project all you'll need is one board of 1 by 8 pine. Pine is an inexpensive softwood that's available almost anywhere. The actual project requires less than five feet of length, but I'd get an eight-foot board just to give you some room for errors. You should note that 1 by 8 inches is the "nominal" dimension of the board. After the wood is milled, it is planed down to a smooth finish, and its actual dimensions are $3/4$-inch thick and $7 1/4$-inch wide.

• *Nails.* You'll need 1½-inch, 4D finish nails. Thinner, wire brads will also work, but they bend easily and are less forgiving for beginners. You'll need about forty to fifty to allow for waste and practice.

BASIC TECHNIQUE

The Principles

We're going to build a very simple wooden box. It's about as easy a project as you can do, but it teaches the necessary skills to do more complicated things. With that said, prepare yourself and your kid for less than perfect results. I can guarantee that you'll make some mistakes. But in the end your kid will have made something with her own hands, and that's something to be proud of. If you have that attitude, so will she.

All of the tasks below can be done by children, but they may need some assistance. Sawing and hammering are unfamiliar motions, and their arms are likely to tire quickly. Stop often for rest or take turns as needed.

With any building project, the fundamentals are the same. Have a plan and know it from beginning to end before you start. Work slowly and methodically, one step at a time. Measure precisely and double-check everything.

Measuring and Marking

Most people don't think of measuring as a carpentry skill, but if it's not done properly, there's no tool in the world that can fix it.

With a sharp pencil and a ruler or measuring tape, place a light mark at the edge of the board, ten inches from the end. Double-check for accuracy. In a small project like this one, even an eighth-inch dif-ference will be noticeable.

Take your carpenter's square (or whatever you're using as your 90-degree angle) and line it up with the long edge of the board. Place the tip of the pencil on the mark you made at ten inches and slide the square over until it just touches the tip of the pencil. Double-check to make sure the square or book is lined up with the edge of the board, then draw a line along the other side of the square all the way across the board. You can double-check the squareness of the line by making sure it's exactly ten inches from the end of the board at both ends.

Sawing

We'll start by making a few practice cuts. The first will be along the line you just marked at ten inches. Don't worry about wasting wood—we'll use this and all the other scrap pieces we cut for other things.

Step 1: Positioning

Place the board on a sturdy bench or across two chairs so the end sticks out beyond the cutting line. The board should be about thigh-high on the person who's sawing. Too high and you'll lose the advan-tage of gravity; too low and it will strain your back. You should be able to bend over and lean on the board with your free hand to brace it. Your cutting arm should line up with the cut so the elbow can move freely back and forth beside you in a straight line.

Step 2: Notching

This is by far the most dangerous part of the project. Check the drawing for proper hand position and proceed carefully.

Have your child place the palm of her hand next to the pencil line and bend the thumb so the tip of the knuckle is just above the line. The rest of the fingers can curl over the edge of the board, where they won't be in the way. The tip of the thumb should be braced against the board and curled away from the line.

Carefully place the saw on top of the line so that when it's lined up properly, it just rests against the knuckle of the thumb. Have your child sight down the saw to make sure it isn't tilted, and to keep it aligned with the pencil mark. The tip of the saw should angle downward at about 45 degrees.

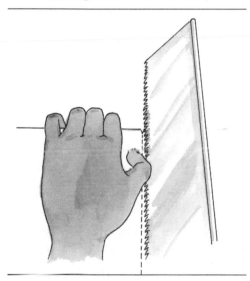

Using the knuckle of the thumb as a guide, have your child *pull* the saw across the edge of the board, cutting a shallow notch right into the pencil line. The saw will try to bounce around, so it's important to pull straight back and to keep the knuckle nice and steady. After several pulls, the notch should be deep enough (about a quarter inch) to get the saw started in the right place.

Step 3: Cutting

Once the notch has been made, have your kid move her free hand away from the pencil line. She should still use that hand to hold the board steady, but it should be well out of harm's way.

Even with a notch, the first few forward strokes will be a little jumpy. Tell your kid to take short strokes, with just the weight of the saw to hold the blade down. Once the blade is staying in its groove, have her lengthen her stroke and begin to bear down as she pushes forward.

Stand either directly in front of or behind her so you can help her sight along the saw. Try to correct any leaning or curving immediately—once the cut veers off in the wrong direction, it's difficult to correct. If the saw begins to wander off line, it should be tipped back to a more horizontal angle to establish a groove right along the pencil mark. Blow away any sawdust that obscures the line. Once things are back on track, the tip of the saw can be tilted downward again. The more downward the stroke, the quicker it will cut.

Once the cut is started, every stroke should be long and smooth. If the blade starts binding against the wood, it's usually tilting or veering away from the established groove.

Step 4: Finishing the cut

When the cut is about an inch from being finished, flip the board over and use a straight edge to draw a line to where the cut is headed. Notch that edge of the board with the same technique you used to start the cut. This will keep that edge from splintering on the last few strokes.

Flip the board back over and finish cutting. As she nears the edge, have your child use short strokes with minimal pressure. Support the piece you're cutting off so it doesn't break off and fall to the ground.

You can use this first scrap piece as a straight edge and to measure 90 degree angles. You can also use it in place of your thumb to guide the saw while notching future cuts. Cut off a couple more pieces of wood for practice, making each of them about three inches long. We'll use these later to practice hammering, and as sanding blocks.

Step 5: Cut your pieces

Now it's time to make some real cuts to make the pieces for our project. Here's what you'll need:

4 pieces: 8¾-inch long (for top, bottom, and two long sides)
3 pieces: 5¾-inch long (for lid insert, and two short ends)

After you've cut one piece, you can use it as a template to measure others of the same size. Don't make all your pencil marks at once and then cut them—the cut itself has width, so you'll end up with slightly shortened pieces. When you're done cutting, set aside the pieces and go on to hammer and nails.

Nailing

Step 1: Positioning

When children pick up an adult-size hammer, they usually try to grip it high on the shaft, right near the head. This gives them a lot of control, but it takes away the force of gravity on the hammerhead. You'll have to fiddle around to find the best place for each child to grip the handle. Closer to the head gives more control, and closer to the end gives more power.

To start, have your child grip the hammer along the side of the handle at about the halfway point, so that the V between the thumb and index finger is on top. The grip should be firm, but not so tight that it keeps the wrist from moving freely.

Stack two pieces of scrap wood on a sturdy surface a little lower than your kid's waist level. Too low is better than too high, because she can lean over to compensate. Put the wood in front of her swinging arm, rather than in front of her belly button.

Have her take a nail and hold its point against the scrap wood. She should grip it with thumb and index finger, as close to the point as possible, and keep it vertical. When she places the face of the hammer on the head of the nail, its surface should be level with the ground. Her elbow should hang at her side in a relaxed position, and the handle of the hammer should be horizontal.

Last, but not least, make sure you are both wearing your safety glasses.

Step 2: Swinging the hammer

The position described above is the one the hammer should be in as it strikes the nail. The trick is getting there with both power and accuracy.

For children just starting out, the hammering motion should come from the wrist. Later on, as they get more comfortable, they'll add a little elbow for more power. Think of the hammer and hand as a wooden arm at a railroad crossing. It pivots at the wrist, but it doesn't move back and forth or side to side. Most important, the wrist never drops below the point where it can hold the hammer horizontal as it strikes the nail.

Have your child start out with little taps on the nail head. She should keep her eye on the head of the nail and keep her wrist at the same height at all times. Don't let her raise and drop her arm and try to *push* the nail in. The motion should be relaxed and fluid. It's a lot like wagging your finger at a naughty pet.

There's no need to pound the nail—all your child has to do is lift the head up, then guide it down through exactly the same arc, letting gravity do its work. Once the nail is in far enough to stand on its own

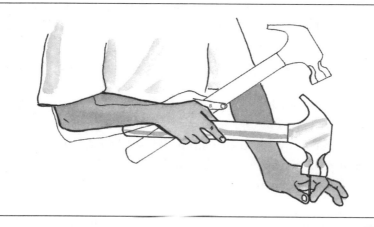

(about a quarter-inch deep), she can move her free hand away and swing with more force. This is done by lifting the hammerhead a little higher—*not* by swinging harder. If she starts putting a little elbow into it, that's fine, so long as the strikes are still accurate and the wrist doesn't drop down too low as she makes contact.

If the nail starts to bend, it's usually because of an off-center hit, or because the face of the hammer is not level as it strikes the nail. Catch bends as soon as they begin, and correct them by tapping the nail straight from the side. If the nail is bent beyond saving, use the "claw" on the back of the hammer to pull it out and start again. If the child keeps bending nails, check her wrist position and go back to small taps, working back up to bigger swings slowly.

Step 3: Finishing up

When the nail head is almost all the way in, have your child slow down and concentrate on very accurate strikes. The last few should be light taps. Any miss-hits at this point will dent the board. When the nail head is exactly level with the surface of the wood, it's time to stop.

Check the other side of the bottom piece of scrap to see if the nail penetrated. You'll need this information later.

Assembling the Box

Take all four of your 8¾-inch pieces and stack them together. Wrap a piece of the coarse sandpaper around one of the 3-inch scrap pieces and use it to take off any protrusions. Be careful—pine is very soft, so coarse sandpaper takes the wood off quickly. Use it to even up the boards, making them the same size, and correct any crooked or slanted cuts.

Compare your 5¾-inch pieces and set the smallest one aside as your lid insert. Stack the other two and sand them as above, until they are as similar as possible.

Hold the pieces together to see how they fit.

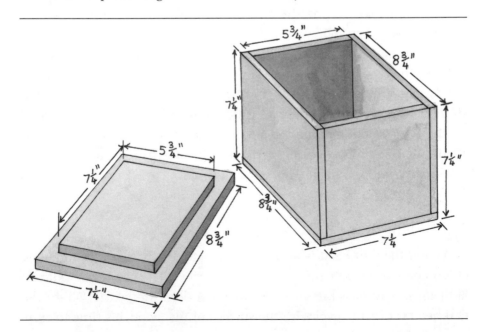

Once you know where everything goes, take one of the long side pieces and place it on top of your 10-inch piece of scrap wood. Use a straight edge to draw a faint line three-eighths of an inch from each end. Hammer three nails—one at the top, one at the bottom, and one in the middle—halfway into the board at each of these lines, until their points just penetrate to the other side.

Stand the two, short end pieces on edge so they support the long piece with the nails. Hammer the nails through into the edges of the end pieces, forming a little table. Flip these three joined pieces over. Prepare the other long side piece as you did the first one, with nails hammered halfway through, then nail it onto the upright end pieces. You should now have a box that's open on either side.

Prepare the bottom piece as you did the two long pieces, this time placing three nails along each of its four sides, three-eighths inch from the edge. Nail it onto the bottom of the box, which should now be open on only one side.

Take the remaining short piece and sand down its edges until it fits easily into the opening at the top of the box. Center it carefully on the top piece and nail it in place, forming a lid. If your nails penetrated the double thickness of scrap board when you were practicing with the hammer, take care not to drive these nails all the way down.

Place the lid on the box. With the lid in place, use coarse sandpaper to round off corners and sharp edges, and to smooth over hammer dents and irregularities in the joints. Use the fine sandpaper to give a smooth finish to the entire surface of the box.

WHAT'S NEXT

If you leave the wood bare, it will pick up stains and marks. To protect it, apply a couple of coats of water-based urethane. It's easy to use, and relatively nontoxic. If you'd like to decorate the box before coating it, try painting on a design with a little wood stain. Use a small artist's brush, and keep it simple. If you stain too large an area, pine is a wood that will look splotchy, and all the scratches and dents will show.

SAFETY TIPS

The best protection when using tools is to use them properly. Use good technique, and never use a tool for a purpose for which it wasn't intended. When not in use, keep them out of reach of younger children.

For hammering, a pair of safety glasses is a good idea. A miss-hit nail can become a projectile, and beginners make a lot of miss-hits.

YEAH, BUT HOW IS HE WITH A RADIAL ARM SAW?

Our ancestors first started to make their own tools about three and a half million years ago. This has long been considered a great development in human history, one that differentiated us from other animals on Earth. However, in 1991 a male chimpanzee named Kanzi showed us that we might not be so different after all.

Scientists taught Kanzi to use sharp stones to slice the strings off of a box, allowing him to open it and get a reward. Next, they taught him to smash stones apart and search for a piece with a sharp edge. Eventually he learned to strike one stone against another like a hammer, creating sharp fragments that he could use as tools. This is very close to the kind of crude stone tools that our distant ancestors first learned to make.

I'd hate to see him get loose in Home Depot.

WHAT IS GRAIN?

The swirls and patterns in a piece of wood are called its grain. When we cut across the trunk of a tree, we see these alternating zones of dark and light as rings. As a tree grows, it lays down new wood just below its bark. In the spring and summer it forms cells that move sap and water. In the winter it lays down denser cells, meant mainly for support. By counting the rings, we can find out how many years a tree has lived.

To make boards, tree trunks are cut lengthwise, so their grain appears as lines instead of rings. The cells in a piece of wood are long and hollow, and they run in the same direction as the grain. This gives the wood an unusual property—it has different strength in different directions. To understand why, try this experiment with a box of drinking straws.

Take a handful of straws and lay them on the table, side by side in a single layer. If they have those little bendy places with the ridges, cut them off—we need straight, smooth cylinders. Now tape the straws together, still in a single, flat layer.

If you move the straws to the edge of the table so that some of them are over the edge, they droop over the side from their own weight. Their structure doesn't provide much strength in that direction. Now, if you rotate the straws 90 degrees so that all of them are hanging halfway over the edge, the structure is much stronger. Still, if you press on them with your finger, you can bend them pretty easily.

Now, stand the straws upright on the table and gather them up into the shape of a tree trunk. Press down on top of them. This is the direction in which they have the greatest strength.

All of this makes perfect sense. A tree must support the tremendous weight of its branches. It must also resist the lesser force of the wind. But there's very little in nature that would split a tree along its grain.

The next time you see someone splitting boards in a martial arts demonstration, try to get a look at the wood. I guarantee they won't be splitting it end on, or across the grain. They'll be splitting it *along* the grain, where every board is weakest.

THE WORLD'S BIGGEST HAMMER

In Eureka, California, there's a real wood and metal hammer that holds up the sign for a building supply store. It's fourteen feet long.

STUPID CARPENTRY JOKES

Q: How did the carpenter break his tooth?
A: Biting his nails.

Q: Why did the carpenter yawn when he went to pick up some wood?
A: He got board.

Q: What kind of saw takes two people to use?
A: A seesaw.

Q: Why did Betty do her homework on sandpaper?
A: It was just a rough draft.

17
SPIN A YO-YO

> *"Being a parent is like being a yo-yo. You're up . . . you're down . . . you're at the end of your rope—but you know you're doing what you were meant to do."*
>
> —*Anonymous*

Ah . . . the Circle of Life. The sun rises and sets. The moon waxes and wanes. The Earth circles the sun each year. And at least once in every childhood, yo-yos make a comeback.

For me, it happened in fifth grade. They seemed to appear overnight, and within days every kid in my class had one. The teachers had to ban them from the classroom, under threat of confiscation. And out at recess, the playground flashed with color as the little orbs dipped and whirled on the ends of their strings.

The craze reached its frenzied peak when the Duncan Yo-Yo Champion came to town. I'm still not sure how he got to be champion, but at the time it didn't matter. We couldn't have been more excited if President Nixon himself had dropped by.

The crowd at the playground was larger than the organizers had expected. They had to keep telling people to back up and give the champ a little room. I climbed up on the jungle gym with about twenty other kids and craned my neck to get a better view. I wasn't disappointed.

He was the champ all right. There was no doubt about it. Rock the Baby, Walk the Dog, Around the World—the names of the tricks were as colorful as his yo-yos. He kept two of them going at all times, even when he was talking. They whirled around his hands in tight orbit, like little comets circling the sun at his command. After the demonstration, he signed yo-yos for anyone who bought one of his special Championship Edition models. I bought one with three months of allowance and waited in line. When I got to the front, he shook my hand, as if I was a grown-up.

"How's it goin'?" he asked. "Are you getting any of those tricks down?"

"Not yet," I said.

"Practice," he said. "All it takes is practice."

I nodded solemnly and walked away with my prize.

That summer, I worked on yo-yo tricks every day, and by the time school started again, I was pretty good. I brought my championship model on the first day, ready to show off my newfound skill. The only problem was, no one cared. Yo-yos weren't in anymore. Like seventeen-year locusts, they had emerged into the sunlight for a brief moment, only to vanish as quickly as they came.

I'm not sure what the life cycle of the yo-yo is, but I do know one thing. Sometime during my kids' childhood years, yo-yos will be back. When they get here, I'll be ready.

WHEN TO START

Most six-year-olds can handle the basic drop and return, but a lot of the tricks require more coordination. For fancy stuff, hold off until seven or eight.

CHOOSING A YO-YO

In the old days, Duncan Yo-Yos dominated the market. They had a few basic models and a "butterfly" model for string tricks. You pretty much just found one in the color you liked and you bought it.

Nowadays there are all sorts of brands with every imaginable high-tech feature. They have flashing lights, and bells and whistles, and special, trick axles. Call me old school, but I'll take my good old Duncan Imperial any day. It's not fancy, but it gets the job done.

Whatever model you buy, don't go for the cheap knock-off at the bottom of the display. Inexpensive yo-yos tend to be too light and poorly balanced. Even worse, they have cheap strings that haven't been properly wound. As you'll soon discover, the string is almost as important as the yo-yo.

It's probably best to buy two—one for you and one for your child—since the string needs to be trimmed to fit the user.

BASIC TECHNIQUE

Step 1: String management

When you first unwrap your child's yo-yo, let it unwind completely and dangle it so that it just touches the floor. Cut the string at a spot three or four inches above your kid's belly button.

Double the last couple of inches of the string and tie it in a knot, creating a small, fixed loop. Pull the knot tight and trim off the loose end. Then draw the string through the loop, creating a slipknot that's easily loosened.

Before you rewind the string, notice how it attaches to the axle. It isn't tied on tightly. Instead, it loops around the axle and twists back onto itself. In good quality yo-yos, the string is wound in such a way that the twist is stable, exerting no torque on the yo-yo when you let it hang suspended in the air. Cheap yo-yos have to be wound tighter or they become too loose at the axle. This causes knots to appear anytime the string is loose, and it's a constant source of frustration.

To rewind the string, wind it loosely around the axle several times until it begins to catch. After that, wind it with a small amount of tension, just enough to avoid loose loops.

Step 2: The drop and return

Place the slipknot around the middle finger and pull it snug. I like to put it around the middle knuckle, but some people like the feel of it farther out or in.

Wrap the middle finger around the center groove of the yo-yo, and let the index and ring fingers curl up on either side. Hold the yo-yo in front of the body with the hand palm down, at about belly-button level.

With a smooth, downward flick of the wrist, release the yo-yo and send it straight down. Before it reaches bottom, move the hand upward until you feel the tug of the yo-yo reaching the bottom of the string. There's no need to jerk on the string with any force—a smooth upward motion works better. Then, as the yo-yo returns, lower your hand to meet it at belly-button level. At that point you can either grasp it or send it down for another spin.

Some kids can pick up the motion just by watching and experimenting, but most will catch on faster if you place your hand over theirs and move it for them to demonstrate the timing.

Step 3: The wrist whip

The drop and return is pretty passive. To get a sense of control over the yo-yo, you need to give it more spin and velocity. This calls for a different technique.

Turn your hand palm up and bend the elbow and wrist so the yo-yo is at the center as your hand and arm spiral around it. Don't forget to grip the yo-yo with the middle finger around the groove and the index and ring fingers on either side. Check the string, and make sure it winds from your finger over the top of the axle, rather than underneath it. This allows the yo-yo to spin out of your hand in the direction that unwinds it.

With a quick, smooth motion, flick the forearm and the wrist downward. The elbow unbends only to about 90 degrees, and the fingers point away from you. As the yo-yo spins off the end of your fingers, flip your hand over so it's palm down, and lift it until the yo-yo tugs and starts to return. Just as before, lower your hand and catch it at belly-button level. It'll move a lot faster than it did with the simple drop, so it might take a while to get the timing.

It's important to send the yo-yo straight down, so the string doesn't push against the sides of the groove. It also helps to get as much spin as possible. That's because a yo-yo is another example of a gyroscope (like the wheels of a bicycle, or a Frisbee). The more it spins, the more stable it is, and the more likely it is to stay in the right position.

Step 4: Sleeping

If you send the yo-yo spinning downward but don't lift your

hand as it hits bottom, it may return anyway, but with less force. On the other hand, it may get to the bottom and just spin there. This is called "sleeping," and it's the basis for all kinds of tricks. The more spin you have, the longer the yo-yo will sleep. When you want it to return, just give the string a tug, and the yo-yo should zip back to your hand. Once again, it's important to send the yo-yo straight down, so the string doesn't rub against the sides of the groove.

Your yo-yo will sleep more easily if you untwist the string a little, loosening its grip on the axle. Don't overdo it, though. If it's too loose, it won't return.

Step 5: The quick-wind

Here's a fast way to wind the string onto your yo-yo. Hold your string hand high enough so you can reach the yo-yo with the other hand. Place your index and middle fingers on either side of the groove, with the string coming out between them. In this position, pull the string taut between your two hands. Then push your fingers downward so they roll off the yo-yo, imparting as much spin as possible. The yo-yo will climb partway up the string, and with a few more drops and returns, it should make it all the way to your hand.

TROUBLESHOOTING

Twisted

Sometimes, in the course of doing tricks or just from winding the string, you end up with too much twist. You can tell this is the problem because whenever the string is loose, it coils itself up into little knots. You may also find that the yo-yo stops sleeping, because the extra twist makes the string too tight around the axle. The solution is simple—let the yo-yo hang by its string until it untwists itself.

The Big Sleep

Sometimes the string loosens to the point where the yo-yo just sleeps and won't return. This usually means too little twist. It can happen while winding the string, or sometimes just by doing a long series of wrist whips. The solution is the same as for too much twist. Let the yo-yo hang and rotate back to neutral. If necessary, you can even add a little more twist, but don't add enough to knot the string.

The Tilt

When the yo-yo keeps tilting to one side and tangling up in its string, there can be many causes. Sometimes the yo-yo is poorly balanced or the string is too twisted. On the other hand, you may simply be releasing it in a tilted position. Check the grip and make sure the yo-yo's groove lines up with the middle finger. For wrist whips, make sure the string winds from the finger over the top of the axle, not the bottom. Finally, try aiming your wrist whip at different spots on the floor. Some people prefer to aim at their toes, some out in front, and some off to the side.

WHAT'S NEXT

Once you master the basic wrist whip and the sleeper, there are all sorts of tricks you can try. Here are a couple of easy ones.

Walk the Dog

This is the simplest of the many sleeper tricks. Put the yo-yo to sleep as usual, then lower it gently onto the floor. A rug works better than a slippery surface. The yo-yo should roll forward on the end of its string, as if it's on a leash. Give it a little tug, and it jumps back to your hand.

Around the World

This is one of the easiest loop tricks, also known as an outside loop. Instead of holding the yo-yo in front of you for a wrist whip, hold your arm behind you and off to the side, as if you're about to roll a bowling ball. Turn the palm backward and upward, and grip the yo-yo as usual. Now, as you swing your arm forward, flick the wrist forward and release the yo-yo toward a spot on the floor a few feet in front of you.

The yo-yo will shoot out in front of you, then swing up and return at a level above your hand. Initially, you can just reach up and catch it. Then, when you're more comfortable with the motion, try letting it loop up and around your hand. As it orbits around, follow its flight with a twist of your wrist until it shoots out in front again. When it comes back, you can either catch it or try to loop it again.

THE FIRST YO-YO

The yo-yo probably originated in China many centuries ago, then spread to the rest of Asia, the Middle East, and eventually Europe. The oldest surviving reference is a painting on a Greek vase from around 500 BC. It portrays a Greek boy playing with a yo-yo.

WHY IS IT CALLED A YO-YO?

The yo-yo spread around the world and became very popular with the European aristocracy in the late 1700s. The yo-yo arrived in Paris in 1791, and as it spread through France it was called "le joujou de Normandie," or "the plaything from Normandy." One theory is that the English term *yo-yo* comes from this phrase. However, the more likely source is a place on the other side of the world. The modern yo-yo that was popularized in the United States had its roots in the Philippines. There, the phrase *yo-yo* means "come-come."

AMAZING YO-YO RECORDS

• The record for most consecutive outside loops is fifty-four, by Dale Myberg in 1996.

• The longest sleeper was fifty-one seconds, by Dale Oliver in 1991.

• The world's largest yo-yo weighed 256 pounds and was lowered from a large crane to kick off the U.S. National Yo-Yo Championships in Chico, California, in 1999.

STUPID YO-YO JOKES

Q: What did they call the first musical yo-yo?
A: Yo-Yo Ma.

Q: Why didn't the yo-yo cross the road?
A: He was sleeping.

*   *   *

A woman walked into a toy store with a little boy and asked the salesman: "Can I get a yo-yo for my son?"

"No," he said. "We don't do trades."

18
GROW A GARDEN

"All gardeners live in beautiful places—because they make them so."

—Joseph Joubert

I have a confession. When I was a kid, I liked vegetables. Not *all* vegetables, of course. I hated limp, cafeteria string beans as much as the next kid. But we didn't eat a lot of canned vegetables in my house. We had a garden.

It wasn't fancy—just a big patch of dirt with a chicken wire fence to keep out the woodchucks. But every year, we fed a family of six out of it, and we never opened a can from spring until fall.

As soon as the ground thawed in March, we were out there with our shovels, turning over the soil. The two bigger kids took turns digging, and the little kids collected worms for the next fishing trip. Soon, the first seeds were planted. Every day after school we'd run out back as soon as we got home to scan the rows of dirt for the first hints of green.

Before long we'd be harvesting spinach and lettuce and baby bok choy. The pea vines would climb their trellis like serpents, and we'd explore them with our little hands, searching for the sweet green pods. Then warmer nights would come and so would the radishes and carrots and the long green beans. By midsummer the corn was taller than we were, and the zucchini were so big we could have carved them into canoes. On hot August days, I used to walk out to the garden with a salt shaker in hand, looking for the perfect tomato with my name on it.

Years later, when my wife and I bought our first home, I meant to start a vegetable garden right away. But when our first daughter came along, our more ambitious projects got pushed to the back burner.

One day, I remember trying to convince her to eat some green peas.

"Come on, honey, veggies are good. They help you grow up big and strong."

She knocked the spoon out of my hand and sent peas flying all over the kitchen.

"I don't want them!" she said. "I *hate* veggies!"

The next morning, I walked outside and started to dig up our yard.

WHEN TO START

A vegetable garden is a great project for kids of any age. Our youngest was picking snow peas when she was only two. So as long as your kid is old enough to be around a bunch of dirt and manure without eating it, you can give it a try.

WHAT YOU NEED BEFORE YOU START

A Patch of Dirt

What are the three most important things to remember in real estate? Location, location, location. The same goes for a garden.

Vegetables love sunlight. Almost everything else can be brought in from somewhere else, but the spot you choose has to get light—preferably at least four hours of direct sunlight every day. Water is also important. Plant your garden within a hose length of a tap, or you'll have to do it by hand. A full watering can weighs about thirty pounds, and vegetables can get very thirsty. Enough said.

The last thing to think about is your soil. Of course, rich, moist, loamy soil is ideal, but it's almost impossible to find. Luckily, even the worst soil can be improved. You can minimize how much work that takes by staying away from places with large rocks and roots. Also be wary of soil contaminants. A spot beside a busy street can collect lead, and some soils contain toxins from previous industrial use.

If you can't find a suitable spot, don't give up. You can build a deep raised bed and bring in your own soil, or just use large pots and containers instead.

Tools and Equipment

For a small garden, a spade and a rake are the only tools you absolutely need. Get the best quality you can afford. Cheap tools break easily and end up costing you more in the end. You may also want some small hand tools, like a trowel and a claw, and maybe a long-handled weeding tool, like a hoe.

Besides tools, you'll need gardening gloves (in adult and kid sizes), some old shoes and work clothes, and a soft-spray nozzle or watering wand that fits on your hose.

Soil Amendments

The key to creating good soil is organic material. It keeps sandy soil moist, and it lightens clay soils so they can drain. It also adds nutrients that plants need to grow. Whatever you use should be well rotted before you use it. Rotten leaves, compost, worm castings, and composted manure are all good choices. Peat moss lightens the soil nicely, but it's expensive and acidic. If you use it in a vegetable bed, you'll need to add a little lime to make the soil slightly alkaline, the way veggies like it.

If you plan to use fresh manure or grass clippings, let them rot first. Also avoid sawdust—it robs the soil of nitrogen. Finally, you can improve drainage in heavy clay soils by adding some sand.

Fertilizer

Ideally, a lot of your plants' nutritional needs will be met by your soil amendments. A healthy dose of manure or compost can eliminate the need for other fertilizers entirely. But if you plan on making efficient use of a small garden space, a little extra fertilizer won't hurt.

Different plants need a different balance of nutrients. Leafy plants, like lettuce, use more nitrogen. Root crops, like carrots, need phosphorus. And fruiting plants, like tomatoes, use more potassium. You can find special fertilizers to meet these needs, but a well-balanced, general formula for vegetables works fine.

Organic fertilizers provide the same nutrients as chemical fertilizers, but they come from natural sources, such as ground fish or animal bones. They tend to release their nutrients slowly, so they're less likely to "burn" the roots of your plants. Long-acting fertilizers do much the same thing, and some of them continue to work for up to four months.

Seeds and Starts

Vegetable seeds can be found at almost any garden store or nursery. They come in little envelopes with pretty photos and tempting descriptions. In the same stores, you'll also find racks of vegetable "starts." These are small plants that have already been started in little pots. The bigger the plant, the more it'll cost.

It doesn't matter that much what brand of seed you buy unless you live in an unusual climate. In those cases, your nursery may carry special hybrids that do well in your particular area. If you decide to plant starts, try to find healthy specimens with no signs of stress or disease. Avoid plants that have outgrown their pots, looking spindly and falling over under the weight of their own leaves.

When you're deciding which vegetables to plant, there are several things to consider. First of all, what does your kid eat? Later on I'll suggest some crops that most kids like, but everyone's taste is different. Still, don't be afraid to try an experiment or two. Garden fresh vegetables are much tastier than their store-bought equivalents, and if your children help grow and harvest them, they may suddenly start eating things they would have shunned before.

Another factor to think about is climate. Some crops thrive in cold weather and can be planted as soon as the ground thaws. Others do well in the heat, but wither with even the lightest frost. Each seed package will list proper planting time, days until harvest, and any special needs. Plant a mixture of cold and warm weather crops so you can harvest over many months.

BASIC TECHNIQUE

Step 1: Prepare the bed

Choose a bed size that matches not only your ambition but your time and energy. Remember, a 4 by 4 foot garden has nearly twice as much area as a 3 by 3 one, and it'll be twice as much work. If this is your first garden, you might try a bed that's about 4 feet wide and 6–8 feet long. It will provide a surprisingly large crop, but it shouldn't overwhelm you.

I'd recommend raising the surface of the bed six to twelve inches above ground level. This provides better drainage, and the soil will warm up earlier in the spring, allowing a longer growing season. It also requires less bending, and the sides can serve as seats while you weed or do other work.

You can build the bed by surrounding it with wood, concrete blocks, brick, or stone. This gives a nice, finished look, and it helps keep little feet from trampling delicate plants. You may want to avoid treated wood—although it lasts longer, there may be a risk of toxins leaching into the soil and getting into your food.

For our purposes, I'll describe a bed with sloping sides and no retaining wall. This design gives you less planting area but takes less work.

• Start by driving four stakes into the ground for corners and marking off the area with twine. If possible, make the garden run east to west so the plants are less likely to shade each other as the sun traverses the sky to the south. Use your spade to cut straight down along the entire perimeter, then slice off the top layer of grass or weeds. Removing turf is a tough job, so take your time and work with small pieces. If you want to, you can stack the turf upside down and cover it with black plastic. In a few months the grass and roots will break down and you'll be left with topsoil.

• Once you uncover the soil, you need to break it up so your vegetables' roots can penetrate and grow. When you start a garden from scratch, it's a good idea to loosen the soil as far down as you can. The best method for this is "double-digging."

Dig a trench along one edge of the garden, shoveling the dirt into a wheelbarrow or onto a tarp. At the bottom of the trench, loosen the soil by digging deeper and turning it over in place, then breaking up any clods. If you're adding soil amendments, put some into the bottom of the trench. Now step back and dig the next row, dumping each shovelful into the initial trench and breaking it up. Now you've created a new trench. Turn and loosen the bottom, just as before, add your soil amendments, then step back and start all over again. When you reach the end of the garden, take the load of dirt from the first trench and use it to fill in the last row.

• At this point, you'll notice that the surface of the bed is a good deal higher than the ground level. This is due to the amendments you added, but also to the loosening of the soil. Add another layer of amendments to the top of the bed and spread it out with your rake, taking care to break up clods of dirt. Remove any rocks bigger than an inch across, and line them up around the bed to help mark the border. Raking soil, breaking clods, and moving around rocks are all great activities for kids who aren't strong enough to dig.

• Once the soil and amendments are well mixed, shape your bed with a flat top and a 45-degree slope at the sides and ends. Leave a little trench around the edges to capture water that runs off the sloping sides. From this point on make sure no one steps on the surface of the bed. You want the soil to stay loose and aerated all year around.

Now, stand back and admire your work. Congratulations! You've just constructed a raised garden bed. The hardest work is done—now come the fun parts, which are also the easiest parts in which to involve your kids.

Step 2: Make a plan

Before you put in starts and seeds, put some thought into the layout of your garden. It's a good idea to make a drawing of your bed and sketch out a garden plan. Check seed packets and planting directions for the space, sunlight, and planting time needed for each crop. Arrange your plants so they won't shade one another, with taller plants on the north side of the bed. When planting cool weather crops, leave room for the warm weather plants that will go in later.

Once you're done, file away your plan for later reference. You'll want to have it next year so you can rotate crops as a way of avoiding pests (see below).

Step 3: Plant your garden

Vegetables can be divided into two basic categories: cool weather plants and warm weather plants. Breeding can create hybrids that stretch the growing season in one direction or the other, but only so far. Cold-loving plants, like lettuce and spinach, do well in the cool, moist climate of springtime, but may bolt—produce flowers and seeds—in the warm weather, and become bitter. On the other hand, warmth-loving plants like tomatoes can be killed by a late frost, or may simply grow poorly if planted too early. The first rule of planting is to choose the right time of year for each particular plant.

SEEDS

You can buy seeds ahead of time as long as you keep them in a cool, dry place. Make sure you read the instructions on the seed packet before you plant, paying special attention to depth, spacing, and planting season.

Most of the time, seeds are planted at a depth only two or three times their diameter. For tiny seeds, like lettuce or carrot, only a light covering of fine soil or peat moss is needed—just enough to keep them from drying out. Try to space seeds far enough apart so they will grow as individual plants rather than clumps. This will make it much easier to thin them later on. The subtleties of planting depth and spacing tend to be lost on younger kids, so supervise them closely. A handful of seeds dropped in a pile will give a less than satisfactory crop.

Once the seeds are planted, keep the top layer of soil moist (not soaked) until the plants have sprouted and are well established. This is the most vulnerable time in the plant's life, especially to any kind of drought. Once they sprout, a dilute, liquid fertilizer will help them get off to a good start.

STARTS

Unless you live in a mild climate, you won't want to plant warm-weather vegetables as seeds. By the time the harvest comes, you may lose the seeds to the first frost. Instead, plant vegetables that have already been started in pots and grown under protected conditions.

You can grow your own starts, but it's a lot of work for a first garden. It's probably better to buy them at a nursery or garden store. When you get them home, put them in your garden space with their pots half buried for a couple of nights, so they can get used to the temperature and conditions there. Keep their soil moist until you get them planted.

If possible, pick a cloudy day to transplant them, or plant them in the late afternoon. Water each start, and let it drain any excess water.

Dig a hole that's a little bit wider and deeper than the pot, and sprinkle in a little fertilizer. You can add some slow-release fertilizer as well, if you want to cut down on feedings later on. Mix the fertilizer into the soil so it won't burn the delicate roots.

With a butter knife, separate the sides of the pot from the roots and soil. Put your hand over the top of the pot, with the stem of the plant between your fingers. Turn the pot over and tap the bottom gently until the root ball slips out into your hand. Without disturbing the roots, place the plant in the hole and fill in the spaces around it with dirt. Pat the soil gently to stabilize the plant. Form a little wall around the outside of the hole to hold the water in place, then water thoroughly.

For the first week after planting, make sure the soil stays moist and shield the plant from intense heat or sunlight. Don't worry if it looks a little droopy at first—most starts go through some transplant shock, and most survive it.

Step 4: Care and feeding

Once your seeds have sprouted and your starts have adjusted to their new home, the work of a vegetable garden changes pace. Now, the hectic task of planting gives way to the daily chores that keep your garden lush and productive all season long. This is when gardening becomes a kind of meditation. Every morning, you and your child can go out to water the crops and survey the land. When you come home, you can pick out a weed or two and bring in an armful of fresh veggies for dinner. A garden is a source of daily care and daily pride. It's a gift—one worth passing on to your kids.

WATERING

As your plants grow, their roots reach deeper and become less vulnerable to drought. Now you can water less frequently, but each watering needs to be thorough. When the soil feels dry to the touch an inch below the surface, it's time to water. Don't wait until the plants start to wilt.

Use a gentle spray from a nozzle or a watering wand to avoid washing soil away from the roots. Make sure to moisten the soil at least three or four inches below the surface. If it's hot and sunny, water early or late in the day. Watering in the full afternoon sun can burn the leaves of the plants. I prefer to water in the morning, if possible. It fortifies the plants for the stress of the midday heat, and it doesn't leave moisture overnight that can attract pests and disease.

If you don't want to water by hand, a drip hose and a timer do a great job of watering deeply without losing a lot to evaporation. Set the timer conservatively at first—overwatering can drown the plants and rot their roots.

WEEDING

If you want your crops to thrive, you have to wipe out their competition. That means weeds. When they're small, just pull them out by the roots before they get started. But if you've got a big garden or a sore back, use a long-handled hoe to cut the weeds off at ground level. While you're at it, scuff up the surface of the soil to help it absorb water. Do a little every day, and it won't feel like a chore. Better yet, do it with your child. Many a heart-to-heart talk has started with a little time, a little sunshine, and a few pesky weeds.

THINNING

Weeds aren't the only competition for your crops. When vegetables are planted too close together, there aren't enough nutrients in the soil to go around. This is why planting instructions always tell you how far apart to space the plants. But when you plant seeds, you can't be sure how many will germinate. The solution is to plant more seeds than you'll need, then thin them to the proper spacing when the plants are established. Pick out the weaker, smaller plants and cut them off at ground level. Don't yank them out—you'll disturb the roots of their neighbors. If you're thinning lettuce or other greens, the tender young leaves are great eating.

FERTILIZING

As we discussed before, there are all kinds of fertilizers, and most of them will get the job done if they're balanced and meant for general use. Make sure you add some when you plant and during the first few weeks of rapid growth. For fruiting plants (cucumber, tomato, squash, etc.), apply a little fertilizer as soon as the fruit starts to appear. Make sure you follow directions closely. Keep concentrated fertilizers away from direct contact with the plant or its roots, and water thoroughly after it's applied.

MULCHING

Mulch is what you put on top of the soil to block out weeds and prevent evaporation of water. It can be anything from black plastic to hazelnut shells. For vegetable gardens, choose something that will break down quickly and enrich the soil, like dried leaves or compost. Put on at least a couple of inches, especially around warm weather plants that take a long time to mature. It will cut your weeding and watering in half.

FAVORITES

There aren't any hard and fast rules about what to plant in a kid's garden, but here are a few crops that our kids always love.

Peas

In the spring, when most plants are still shivering in their green-houses, peas are already a foot tall and sporting pretty, purple flowers that look like pansies. They are crisp and sweet eaten right off the vine, and harvesting them is a daily treasure hunt. Try snap peas, snow peas, and shelling peas, and see which ones your kids like best. Even the vines are edible, when they're tender and young. Plant the seeds directly in the ground and put up a trellis or fence to support the vines.

Potatoes

Mashed, fried, or baked—potatoes are a reliable kid-food in almost any form. Now's your chance to prove that they don't come from a McDonald's bag. Potatoes are grown from other potatoes. You can use ones that have sprouted in your pantry, but the chunks of seed potato that you buy at the garden store have been treated with fungicide and tend to be more disease-resistant.

One fun way to grow potatoes is in a large container, like a plastic garbage can. Drill some drain holes in the bottom of the can and plant three or four potatoes in a few inches of soil. When the plants are about six inches tall, add more soil until only the top leaves are showing. Keep doing this until the plant and the soil reach the top of the can. Water and feed the plant as you normally would. At the end of summer, when the plant withers and dies, tip over the container. There should be a good-sized crop all the way down to the bottom.

Lettuce

Garden lettuce is sweet, crisp, and easy to grow. Most varieties love cool weather, but some are bolt resistant right into the heat of summer. If your preschooler empties the whole seed packet out at once, you can let the seedlings sprout up densely and eat the thinnings. Once you've thinned down to reasonably spaced plants, harvest the outside leaves one at a time and the plant will continue to produce for weeks. If you're short on planting space, you can also grow most varieties in containers.

Carrots

Make sure you grow at least one root vegetable. There's nothing that kids like better than digging around in the dirt and bringing up dinner! Carrots are the safest choice. They're sweet, colorful, and easy to grow. Plant them from seed early in spring. You can also plant a second crop in July and let it "winter over" right in the garden. Imagine what your kids will say when you take them out to clear away the snow and harvest them for your New Year's dinner.

Cucumbers

Any kid who doesn't like cucumbers probably hasn't tasted fresh ones. For a long, productive harvest, plant them as starts and make sure you pick them while they're still firm and green. If you let them go soft and yellow, the plant will stop producing. You can grow them in a cage or on a low trellis to conserve planting space and to keep the cukes off the ground.

Tomatoes

By the time winter is over and we've eaten Styrofoam tomatoes for six straight months, most of us would kill for a vine-ripened tomato. Resist the temptation to put in too many plants—most modern hybrids bear heavy crops, as long as you care for them properly. Choose quickly maturing varieties, and consider cherry tomatoes and yellow pear tomatoes just for fun. Plant them as starts, after nighttime temperatures are consistently above 50 degrees. Grow them in wire cages, or stake them up to keep them from sprawling all over the ground.

Zucchini

Not every kid loves to eat zucchini, but show them one the size of a cruise ship and you're sure to get an appreciative gasp. They take up a lot of room but they're almost a guaranteed success, and for first-time gardeners, that's a big plus. Pick them young for eating, but let at least one of them grow to titanic proportions, just for fun. The big, orange blossoms are edible too. Try stuffing zucchini flowers with ricotta, then breading them and frying them in olive oil. Yum!

Pumpkins

Need I say more? They take up too much room, but you can train the vine to wander away from the planting space. Once you have a few pumpkins on the vine, prune off the growing end of the plant so that all the energy can go into making future Jack-'o-lanterns.

Corn

This is another crop that takes too much space for most home gardens, but it's too much fun to pass up. There's something about those tall, tasseled stalks swaying in the wind that makes even the worst city slicker feel like Old MacDonald himself. Even if space is limited, plant a few stalks just for kicks. Corn takes a lot of nitrogen out of the soil, so rotate a legume crop like peas or beans into that spot the following year. Legumes extract nitrogen from the air and fix it in the soil.

Strawberries

Imagine your children walking out to the garden through the early morning dew with a bowl of cereal in hand. They peer into a little green mound of leaves and white flowers and pick out a perfectly ripe strawberry to plop on top. We should all start our day so well. Some strawberries bear fruit just once a year, and their berries tend to be larger. But for my money, the smaller, ever-bearing varieties are just as sweet, and more of a good thing. If you don't have room for a few plants in your garden, grow them in a container on a sunny deck.

Edible Flowers

This is an idea whose time has come—and I don't mean just in snooty restaurants. A sprinkling of flower petals makes a salad an event. Frozen in ice cubes, they spruce up even the most mediocre glass of store-bought lemonade. And just growing in your garden or in a container on your front steps, they garnish your life, as well as your meals.

Some good, reliable choices are borage, calendula, nasturtium, marigolds, roses, pansies, and violets. Of course, avoid using pesticides on any flower you might eat.

If you have the space, you should consider growing at least one giant sunflower. With proper feeding, some of them reach more than ten feet tall and have stems that look like little tree trunks. They make you feel like you're gardening in Munchkin Land, and they make a great natural bird feeder at the end of the year.

TROUBLESHOOTING

If you take the time to prepare the bed and plant carefully, and if you're diligent about your watering, weeding, and fertilizing, your garden should do well. Plants want to grow, if you give them half a chance. But once in a while you may run into problems with pests or disease.

There's a different set of dangers lurking for every kind of vegetable—far too many for us to go over here. But here are a few general things you can do to prevent problems.

Rotate Your Crops

Since different plants have different problems, you're asking for trouble if you keep planting the same thing in the same soil year after year. Rotate from one family of vegetables to another. Plant legumes one year (beans, peas), greens the next, and tomatoes or squash the year after that.

Avoid Stressing Your Plants

Inadequate water makes plants weak and vulnerable to disease. Poor nutrition results in poor growth, and deformity or discoloration. Concentrated fertilizers can burn the plant if they come in direct contact with roots or leaves.

Be a Sleuth

Grab a flashlight and check out your garden at night. Kids love this— it makes them feel like private eyes. Most garden criminals do their dirty work under cover of darkness. Look for larvae, slugs, and marauding critters like raccoons.

Hit the Books

For recommendations on specific problems, check out the garden section at your local library or bookstore. There are many books devoted to vegetable gardening, some of which deal only with pests and disease. You can also check out your local Cooperative Extension. These are community-based education programs that were created in partnership with the U.S. Department of Agriculture. They are amazing resources for all kinds of gardening information—especially hard-to-find specifics about local conditions. Look for them in the phone book or on the Internet.

WORM BINS

It's a garbage disposal! It's a bait shop! It's a thousand pets that you never have to take for a walk! What is it? It's a worm bin.

There are lots of methods for making compost. Most of them involve a lot of turning and mixing and watering—but in the end you're rewarded with the best soil amendment and fertilizer money can't buy: compost! It's the gardener's black gold.

But what if I told you there was a simple, easy way to make excellent compost with much less work, and in half the time? It's called a worm bin. Rather than waiting for soil bacteria to break down vegetation, you enlist the help of thousands of earthworms, who eat their way through your garbage and turn it into worm castings. Okay, it's actually worm poop, but you don't have to tell your kids that. Here's how you do it.

Go out and buy a large plastic container with a lid. Using the biggest drill bit you have, drill some drainage holes in the bottom. Fill the container with a "bedding" of shredded paper or dry leaves. Hand-shredded newspaper works fine if the strips are about an inch wide or less.

Now, go to your garden store and buy red earthworms that are specifically meant for worm bins. Other types work, but they eat and reproduce slower. You can also borrow some worms from someone who already has a worm bin, or sometimes you can get them at a bait shop. In a pinch, you can order them online or out of a gardening catalogue.

Water down the bedding until it's moist but not sopping. Put in the worms. Now start adding kitchen waste. Any vegetable waste will do, but avoid meat, eggs, and dairy. Bury it under the bedding and rotate spots. Too nasty a job for you? Let the kids do it. Dirt, slime, creepy-crawlies . . . that's kid heaven! It's the only chore you'll ever see them lining up to do.

Keep the worms moist. They'll work faster in warm weather, but don't let them dry out or they'll bake. When they've gone through all the bedding, stop feeding them for a couple of weeks. Remove a bunch of worms to start the next bin, and dump the remaining castings directly into the garden. It's a complete, gentle fertilizer that improves any soil.

VEGGIE FACTS

Poison in Your Pizza?

Originally, tomato plants grew only in North and South America. At one time they were thought by Europeans to be poisonous, because they belong to the same family as a plant called Deadly Nightshade. Nowadays they're eaten in almost every part of the world.

Peter Piper Picked a Peck of Potent Peppers

Peppers are spicy because of a chemical called capsaicin that is concentrated in their inner walls, white lining, and seeds. The potency of peppers is measured in Scoville Heat Units—named after pharmacist Wilbur Scoville, who developed the grading system. Sweet bell peppers have a Scoville value of 0. Cayenne peppers come in at around 20,000. But the undisputed champ of the pepper world is the habañero. It tops out the Scoville scale at around 350,000.

Big Jack

The largest pumpkin ever grown weighed 1,140 pounds, grown by Dave Stelts of Leetonia, Ohio, in the year 2000. The biggest pumpkin pie on record was more than 5 feet in diameter and weighed more than 350 pounds, but it used only 80 pounds of pumpkin. That means Mr. Stelts's pumpkin could have produced more than fourteen gigantic pies, each of them five feet wide! How would you like to go to *his* house for Thanksgiving?

STUPID VEGGIE JOKES

Q: How do you know carrots are good for your eyes?
A: Did you ever see a rabbit wearing glasses?

Q: Why did the elephant paint its toenails red?
A: So it could hide in the strawberry patch.

Q: What's black and white and green and black and white?
A: Two Zebras fighting over a zucchini.

Q: What did the gardener say to the seed?
A: "I'll cheer for you if you'll root for me."

Q: With what vegetable do you throw away the outside, cook the
     inside, eat the outside, and throw away the inside?
A: Corn on the cob.

*   *   *

Two ripe tomatoes found out they were going to be eaten and decided to escape. They climbed down off their vine and ran as fast as
they could toward the edge of the garden. One of them fell behind,
then tripped and went splat on the ground.

"Hey," said the other one. *"Ketch-up!"*

19
MAKE APPLE PIE

> *"If you want to make an apple pie from scratch, you must first create the universe."*
>
> —*Carl Sagan*

When a four-year-old child plays the violin or calculates square roots in his or her head, it inspires a special kind of admiration. We call these people gifted, as if heaven itself has smiled upon them. My wife Barb is such a person. She has the Gift of Pie.

Until I met her, I scarcely knew what a pie was. In my family, anything we couldn't cook in a wok came from the grocery store in a box. But when Barb made pie, it was a revelation. She could turn out a perfect piecrust with uncanny ability, measuring and mixing ingredients with only her eyes and her hands. With every bite you could hear the angels sing.

Then she lost the gift. It happened during her pregnancy with our first child. Her circulation changed, and her hands grew warm. Suddenly, the crusts weren't coming out right. She kept trying, but nothing seemed to work. One day, after a particularly demoralizing cardboard crust, it was more than she could bear. She wrapped her rolling pin in a clean, white towel and put it away.

Many months later, Barb walked into the house carrying a box of peaches. They were Japanese white peaches, purchased for a king's ransom at the local organic food store. Perfectly round and ghostly pale, each one was wrapped in its own little blanket of protective foam.

"What are those for?" I asked.

"Take the baby and go for a walk," she said.

She pulled out her rolling pin and lifted it from its shroud.

I did as I was told.

When I returned, our house was filled with the smell of ambrosia. On the table was a golden masterpiece of a pie. My wife cut a piece and put it on a plate, motioning for me to sit down. I took a bite. The crust was crisp and tender—its buttery flakes seemed to melt on the tip of my tongue. The peaches were warm and soft, drenched with cinnamon nectar and faintly scented of roses. I wanted that first bite to last forever.

To this day, that pie inspires hushed tones of reverence. It is the pie against which all other pies are judged. But more than that, it was a sign. Heaven was smiling on our home once again. The Gift had returned.

WHEN TO START

When you make a pie, there's a job for everyone. Even little kids can wash apples, blend butter and shortening into flour, sprinkle ice water, mix ingredients, and (with a little help) roll crust. There are a few steps where you'll want to lend a hand, but generally this is a very kid-friendly skill.

WHAT YOU NEED BEFORE YOU START

Equipment

- **An 8- or 9-inch pie plate**

  Nine inches is standard, but 8 makes it easier for little hands to transfer rolled dough. The supplies listed below are enough for the 9-inch pie, so plan to trim off the edges of the crust if you use an 8-inch, and don't overfill the pie. Aluminum pans (not one of the flimsy foil ones) work fine, but clear glass gives the nicest bottom crust.

- **Large rolling pin**

  Heavier ones work best, even for kids, because they require less muscle.

- **Large mixing bowl**

- **Measuring cups, in one-cup and half-cup sizes**

  For measuring flour, these work better than the big, glass measuring cups.

- **Measuring spoons**

- **Paring knife**

- **Pastry blender**

  This is a tool that's shaped like a half-moon, with a straight handle and several curved blades or wires. The ones with stiff, flat blades work best for blending chilled butter. If you can't find one, a butter knife and a fork will do, but they're harder for kids to use.

- **Pastry brush**

- **Waxed paper**

Supplies

For the crust:

2½ cups all-purpose flour

1 teaspoon salt

½ cup (1 stick) unsalted butter, chilled

½ cup solid vegetable shortening, chilled

6 tablespoons ice water

1 tablespoon lemon juice

For the filling:

½ cup sugar (light brown, or half and half dark brown and white)

¼ teaspoon salt

½ teaspoon cinnamon

½ teaspoon nutmeg

2 tablespoons flour

6 medium-sized Granny Smith apples

1 tablespoon lemon juice

1 tablespoon butter

For the glaze:

1 egg white

1 tablespoon water

BASIC TECHNIQUE

Anything that involves a sharp knife or a hot oven should be done by an adult, but your kids can handle the rest. They may need help with rolling and transferring dough, and with sealing the crust.

Basic Principles

Even those of us who lack the Gift can make a good pie if we understand what we're trying to do. Unrolled pie dough consists of globs of fat (butter and shortening) coated with flour and held together with a little water. When you roll out the dough, the fat and flour form layers, which become flaky when baked.

The first key to making good crust is to keep the layers of fat and flour as separate as possible, so it stays nice and flaky. The second is to keep the flour and water from turning into glue. As we go through each step, you'll notice that almost everything we do is meant to achieve one of these goals.

Step 1: Mix the dough

Cold is a pie-maker's best friend. As soon as pie dough begins to warm, the fat melts and seeps into the flour, and the dough will no longer roll out in layers. This was at least part of the problem during my wife's pregnancy, because her hands were always warm. Winter is the perfect season for apple pie—the apples are fresh, the counter is cold, and a warm slice of pie is a singular kind of joy.

Before you start, make sure everything is as cold as possible. The butter and shortening should be chilled, and the water should be as cold as ice. You can even chill the mixing bowl and the pie plate, if your fridge has enough room.

Measure the flour by overfilling the measuring cup and leveling it off with the back of a knife. It's important to get the proportion of fat to flour correct—too much flour makes the dough tough. Add the salt. Cut the chilled butter into half-inch pieces and toss it into the flour.

Using the pastry blender, cut the butter into the flour until the largest pieces are about the size of large peas. (If you couldn't find a pastry blender, cut up the pieces of butter with a knife and mash them with a fork until they get to the right size.) Cut in the shortening, which will be much softer than the butter, until it forms pieces about the size of almonds. Butter tastes better than shortening, but shortening contains much less water, which makes for a nice, tender crust. I like to use half of each.

Combine the ice water with the lemon juice and sprinkle it onto the butter and flour, tossing and mixing it with a fork as you do. Measure carefully! Too much liquid and the dough will be tough, too little and it falls apart.

The acid in the lemon juice keeps the flour and water from forming gluten and becoming tough. Once the water is evenly distributed, stop mixing. The more you mix, the more gluten will form, and the tougher the dough will be. (See *Chapter 6: Bake Bread* for more on gluten.)

Divide the dough into two equal parts and wrap them with plastic wrap, pressing them gently into balls. Place them in the refrigerator and let them rest for at least an hour. We've used as little water as possible, to keep the crust tender. By letting the dough rest, we allow the water to permeate the flour and hold everything together. This also chills the dough, so we can work with it later without it getting too warm.

Step 2: Make the filling

Combine the sugar, salt, spices, and flour, and mix well. White sugar is measured like flour, but brown sugar should be pressed down into the measuring cup until firm. The proportions of ingredients are more flexible for filling than for dough. Some people use more sugar or thickener, some less. You can experiment as you get a feel for what you like.

Peel, core, and cut the apples into thin slices (about a quarter-inch thick). I like Granny Smiths, because they're firm, tart, and available all year. Other firm apples, like Jonathans, Cameos, and Braeburns, will work too, but you may want to double the lemon juice to add tartness.

Toss the apple slices with the lemon juice and then with the sugar mixture until well coated. Put them in the refrigerator to keep them cold. Don't mix up the filling too far in advance—the sugar will pull the juice from the apples, and you'll risk a soggy bottom crust.

Step 3: Make the glaze

Crack an egg over a bowl and carefully pass the yolk back and forth between the two half shells, letting the white drip down into the bowl. Discard the yolk. Separating eggs is a good, basic cooking skill. Let your kids try it, but expect to lose an egg or two before they get it right.

Mix the egg white with the water. This keeps the white from toughening when it's cooked. We'll use this mixture three ways—to patch together broken crust, to keep the filling from soaking into the bottom crust, and to make the top crust shiny and golden brown.

Step 4: Roll out the crust

Try to roll out your pie dough only once. Rerolling is like kneading bread—it forms gluten and toughens the crust. It also ruins the separation of butter and flour.

The best piecrusts are ugly. They fall apart as you move them, and you end up patching them together like Frankenstein's monster. When dough holds together really well, it has too much water and it's guaranteed to be tough. Discuss this fact with your kids, so they don't get discouraged by an ugly pie. Ugly is good!

Remove half the dough from the fridge and unwrap it. Sprinkle a couple drops of water on the counter and spread them around, then put a sheet of waxed paper on the counter and cover it with a thin layer of flour. The water keeps the waxed paper from slipping around. Place the dough on the floured wax paper and press it into a fat disk. Spread a little flour over the top of the dough and on the rolling pin.

Put your kid on a step stool so the working surface is at waist level. Have him roll out the dough a little at a time, starting in the center and rolling toward the edge in different directions. Remind him to spread the dough out evenly, so no spots are too thick or thin, and so the crust stays more or less round.

Keep the rolling pin floured to prevent sticking. You can help by standing behind him and putting your hands on top of his. Try not to press too hard—the weight of the rolling pin should do a lot of the work.

As he continues to roll out the dough, large cracks will develop at the edge of the circle. This is good! The dough is still tender. Trim some excess dough from a part of the disk where it's not needed, and glue it over the crack with a little of the egg white glaze, then sprinkle it with flour and keep rolling. But don't try to patch every little defect. Work quickly, before the dough gets warm. There'll be a chance to do some final repairs before the pie goes in the oven.

When the dough is at least twelve inches in diameter, place the pie plate upside down on top of it. Big hands are an asset for the next step, so you might want to step in and help. Slide one hand under the waxed paper, and hold down the pie pan with the other. In one, smooth motion, flip them both over. Center the crust in the pan and carefully peel off the waxed paper, using a butter knife or spatula if necessary. Trim the edge of the crust so it hangs over the edge of the plate by about a half inch, using any excess to patch up cracks and holes. Put the plate in the refrigerator to cool.

Take out the other ball of dough and roll it onto waxed paper into a twelve-inch disk, exactly as before. Slide it onto a cookie sheet and put it in the refrigerator too.

Step 5: Get the oven ready

Put some foil under the bottom heating element to reflect heat upward and catch dripping juices. Put the rack at the second to lowest level. Preheat the oven to 450°F.

Step 6: Fill the pie

Take the pie plate out of the refrigerator and brush a thin layer of egg white glaze on the bottom crust. Working quickly, layer the apple slices into the crust, packing them closely. You don't need to arrange them in a fancy pattern, but don't leave big air spaces. Dot the top of the filling with a tablespoon of butter.

Now it's time to put the top crust on. Once again, big hands are an asset here, but your child may be able to do it with a little help. The trick is to turn over the crust without letting it break away from the waxed paper in pieces. You don't want to flip it like a pancake— the motion is more like spreading a blanket over a bed.

Lift up the dough, supporting it with both hands under the waxed paper. Let one edge of the disk droop down so it lines up with the edge of the bottom crust. As your hands move across the pie, let the dough and waxed paper slide off gently so they roll into place on top of the apples (see drawing). Center the dough and carefully peel off the waxed paper.

Trim and patch the top crust, using a little egg white glaze as glue.

Roll the edges of the crusts up onto the rim of the pie plate, folding the two layers together and pinching them with your fingers to seal them. The edge should be raised slightly, to keep the juices from over-flowing.

Brush the egg white glaze over the top of the pie, but leave the edges unglazed (they'll brown fast enough on their own). Use the glaze to seal any patches in the top crust. Sprinkle the pie with a little sugar. With a paring knife, cut a few vents in the top crust to let the steam escape. These can be in any pattern you choose—be creative. Cut out your kid's initials, or a snowflake, or a star.

Step 7: Bake

Now you need to go from cold to hot quickly, so the dough will keep its layered structure as it bakes. Place the pie in the middle of the rack, at the second level from the bottom. Bake at 450°F for ten minutes to crisp the crust, then reduce the temperature to 350°F. Make sure you set a timer, or you may end up with a black Frisbee instead of a pie.

Check the pie after it's been at 350°F for about thirty minutes. If the edge of the crust is overbrowned, cover it with a little foil. Keep checking the pie every ten minutes, expecting the total oven time to be about fifty to sixty minutes.

At this point you'll notice that the kitchen is a mess. I find that a pie in the oven is a great motivator for my kids. The rule is simple: no clean-up, no pie. By the time the pie comes out, the kitchen is always spotless.

When the filling is bubbling up through the vents and the crust is golden brown, take out the pie and put it on a wire cooling rack. Let the juices cool and thicken for at least twenty minutes. Serve warm with vanilla ice cream.

TROUBLESHOOTING

Soggy Bottoms

We tried to avoid this problem by brushing some egg white on the bottom crust and by starting with a very hot oven. If that wasn't enough, next time try using the bottom rack of the oven, at least to start with. Also, make sure you bake the pie as soon after it's filled as possible, and use a clear, glass pie plate if you can.

Cardboard Crusts

There are several reasons for tough crusts. The most common are over-mixing, repeated rolling, too much water, and too much flour or not enough fat. Make sure to measure all crust ingredients accurately, and handle the dough as little as possible.

Overflows

This usually comes from overfilling the pie or from not rolling the edge of the crust into a "dam" to hold back the juice. If you remembered to lay a sheet of foil on the bottom of the oven, it shouldn't be too hard to clean up the mess.

Runny Fillings

This happens when there's not enough flour in the filling to thicken the juice from the fruit. Juicy apples may need a little more flour, and berries or peaches will need more still. But don't overdo it—too much flour turns filling into paste.

Hollow Pies

If you pack the filling too loosely, it collapses during the baking, leaving a big air space under the top crust, which then bakes unevenly. Pressing the apple slices down flat instead of just piling them in should solve this.

Crust Catastrophes

Once in a while a crust will refuse to hold together, due to too little water or too much flour. This leaves you with two choices. You can start over, measuring more carefully, or you can attempt a rescue.

To save a crumbling disaster of a crust, break it apart into a bowl. Add one or two more tablespoons of ice water and toss until well mixed. Wrap the dough in plastic wrap and put it back in the fridge for another hour. When you roll it out, it will be sticky, so flour your hands and rolling pin well. This crust will be a little tough, but it won't be bad, and next time you'll do better.

YOU CAN NEVER HAVE TOO MUCH DOUGH

If you used an eight-inch pie plate, you'll have some leftover dough. There's no need to throw it out. You can press it into a miniature crust and fill it with fruit or jam. You can also cut shapes out of it, either freehand or with cookie cutters, and use them to decorate the top of your pie.

Around our house, extra dough transforms into cinnamon twists. Cut the dough into strips, twist them into spirals, coat them with cinnamon sugar, and bake them on a cookie sheet.

SHRUNKEN HEADS

If you have any extra apples, this is a great thing to do with them. Peel the apples and carve them into heads. Don't carve the features too deeply—they'll become much more pronounced as the apple dries. Roll the apples in lemon juice to keep them from overbrowning and to discourage mold. Line the apples up on the windowsill and let them dry. Over the next few weeks they'll turn into grisly, wrinkly, shrunken heads.

WORLD'S LARGEST APPLE PIE

In 1997 the people of Wenatchee, Washington, made the world's largest apple pie. It took more than three hundred volunteers to process 32,000 pounds of apples and 7,000 pounds of sugar and flour. After five hours in a giant, makeshift oven, it weighed in at 38,000 pounds.

"FOUR AND TWENTY BLACKBIRDS, BAKED IN A PIE . . ."

What were those blackbirds doing in there, anyway? Many of the nursery rhymes that we teach our children originated in England hundreds of years ago. Some of them had surprisingly adult themes.

Apparently, the "four and twenty blackbirds," referred to twenty-four monasteries that Henry VIII seized from the Catholic Church after he formed the Church of England. The blackbirds are the black-robed monks.

You might think this is a strange subject for a child's nursery rhyme, but it's not half as bad as some. For instance, "Ring Around the Rosy" is said to be an incantation to ward off the Black Plague, and "Humpty Dumpty" may commemorate the battlefield death and dismemberment of Richard III, the hunchbacked king.

STUPID PIE JOKES

Q: How many apples does it take to make a pie?
A: Apples don't make pies, people do.

Q: How do you stop pastry dough from snoring?
A: Make it turnover.

Q: If you want to be big and strong, should you make your piecrust
   with Crisco or butter?
A: Make it with butter. Crisco is shortening.

A crust and a filling were sitting together alone on the counter.
   "Hey," said the crust, "you're sweet! Let's get together."
   "I don't know," said the filling. "You seem kind of flaky."

20
THROW A FRISBEE

"Studies of flying saucer cults repeatedly show that they are part of a larger occult social world."
—Stupple and McNeece, MUFON UFO Symposium, 1979

Well, it wasn't exactly a cult. It was a co-op dorm at Stanford called Terra. We were kind of a throwback to hippie days gone by. While our fellow undergrads were going to football games and earning their business degrees, we were growing sprouts on the windowsill and talking politics over vegetarian stew.

Our stated values were peace, love, and cooperation, so we disavowed the school's obsession with competitive sports. We imagined ourselves to be above it all. Of course, to survive at Stanford, we had to be just as cutthroat as anyone else. But rather than admit as much by playing traditional sports, we played Ultimate Frisbee.

"Ultimate," as we called it, is a cross between soccer and rugby, played with a Frisbee instead of a ball. We had a pickup game every afternoon, and the competition was fierce. But since we wore bandannas around our heads and played in bare feet and overalls, we figured it must be okay.

Nowadays I don't even pretend I'm not competitive. But I'm still grateful for every moment I've ever spent chasing a Frisbee. It really *is* different from football. Not because it's any less competitive, but because it's just silly enough to keep you honest.

You can't take yourself too seriously when you're flinging around a little flying saucer. For that reason alone it's something everyone should know how to do.

WHEN TO START

It doesn't take much muscle to throw a Frisbee, but it does take coordination. If your kids aren't perfectionists, start them out at around five years old and make sure there isn't anything breakable nearby. On the other hand, if you want them to really master the skill, you might wait until they're six or older.

WHAT YOU NEED BEFORE YOU START

The word *Frisbee* is a registered trademark of the Wham-O Toy Company. There are many similar toys on the market—some of them imitators and others innovators. They come in a variety of materials and sizes, and each has its own advantages. Luckily, the throwing technique is nearly identical for all of them.

To keep things simple, I'm going to stick with the saucer-shaped, plastic disks that most of us grew up with, and I'm going to call them Frisbees, because that's how everyone knows them.

Don't make the mistake of starting your kid out with a cheap, lightweight Frisbee. In general, heavier Frisbees fly farther and are more stable in the air, especially if there's wind. Choose the heaviest disk your child can comfortably throw. For most kids, somewhere between 130 and 140 grams is a good place to start.

BASIC TECHNIQUE

Step 1: The stance

Have your child stand sideways to the direction she wishes to throw, with the shoulder of her throwing arm pointing at the target. Her feet should be a little more than a shoulder's width apart, with her knees slightly bent, and most of her weight should be on her back foot.

Step 2: The grip

Have her grasp the Frisbee along its leading edge—the edge that faces the target. Some people hold a Frisbee with the thumb on top and all the other fingers underneath, but I like to place my index finger along the edge of the disk (see drawing). This gives you a much better feel for the tilt of the Frisbee as you throw it.

The tips of the other three fingers should curl under the disk and press lightly against the inside of the rim, while the thumb presses down from above. The grip should be relaxed, so the wrist stays loose. Using this grip, the thrower should be able to hold the disk more or less level with the ground. If your kid isn't strong enough to do this, have her support the trailing edge of the disk with her other hand.

Step 3: The flick

The reason beginners have problems when they try to throw a Frisbee is that, in reality, you don't throw it—you spin it. In order to have a smooth, stable flight, a Frisbee needs to spin rapidly, and most of the "throwing" motion goes into creating that spin.

Have your kid stand with her elbow close to her body and her wrist flexed inward, so the side of the disk she's grasping is the one farthest from her (see drawing). The Frisbee should almost touch her belly button. Her hand and arm should wrap around the disk, touching its edge with the index finger, the palm, and the forearm. The far edge (the one she's holding) should be a couple of inches lower than the near edge, so that the Frisbee tilts down and away from her.

Now, have her waggle the wrist forward and back a few times, keeping the Frisbee in the same tilted plane. For now, the forearm should move only a little, and the elbow should stay close to the body. Finally, with a quick, smooth motion, have her flick the wrist forward and release the disk, keeping that outside edge tilted down. At the end of the throw, the index finger should point at the target.

Don't worry if the Frisbee doesn't go very far. The purpose of the wrist flick is to create spin. Once she can flick the disk forward into a reasonably straight and stable flight, you can move on to the next step.

Step 4: The shift

Now that your kid can put enough spin on a Frisbee to keep it stable, a little distance can be added to her throws. This time, as she flicks the wrist forward, have her transfer her weight onto the front foot. If she likes, she can take a small step toward the target.

Make sure she doesn't try to add distance by using a big, sweeping arm motion. She needs to snap the wrist, or there won't be enough spin. The power of the throw should come from the legs and the weight of her body, not from the arm.

TROUBLESHOOTING

The Tilt

When a Frisbee is released on a plane that's level to the ground, it doesn't stay that way. Because of its rotation, its inside edge dips downward and it veers off course. This is why you have to compensate by releasing it with the outside edge down. Somewhere between 30 and 45 degrees of tilt is usually needed, depending on the speed and spin of the throw.

The Wobble

A wobbly, unstable throw is due to a lack of spin. Make sure your child keeps the elbow close to the body and snaps the wrist quickly.

The Fizzle

If your kid's throws seem stable but just aren't going anywhere, work on her weight shift. Make sure the shift is simultaneous with the snap of the wrist. If this doesn't work, try a slightly lighter Frisbee.

The Wild Thing

Accuracy is usually a function of follow-through. Make sure your kid's index finger is pointing at the target as she finishes the throw—this keeps her from releasing the Frisbee too early, too late, or too high. Notice that I said the finger—*not the arm*. In a tight, quick, wrist-snap with the elbow held close, the forearm moves very little and comes to a stop before it points at the target (see drawing).

Also, make sure she stays sideways to the target and shifts her body weight forward in the direction she's throwing. If she steps away from the target, or rotates the shoulders as she throws, there'll be Frisbees flying in every direction.

CATCHING

For tips on catching, see *Chapter 3: Catch a Ball.* Many of the same principles apply, and catching a Frisbee tends to be easier because it moves slower and stays on a more level plane. Have your child use two hands at first, but tell her not to squash the disk from the top and bottom as if she's flattening a pancake. She should squeeze the edge of the Frisbee between the thumbs and the fingers, clamping down on it like a vise.

As with catching anything, the most important thing is to watch the Frisbee all the way into the hands. If your kid is flinching, try one of the soft foam or cloth disks, and start out with short, soft tosses.

THE FIRST FRISBEE

In the 1870s there was a pie-maker in Connecticut named William Frisbie. His pies were especially popular with the college students at Yale, who gorged themselves on his creations, then amused themselves by flinging pie tins back and forth among the ivy-covered buildings.

Decades later a man in California named Walter Frederick invented a toy that was meant to mimic a flying saucer. In 1957 he sold his idea to the Wham-O Toy Company. In their search for a name for this new creation, they stumbled across the story of the Yale students and their flying pie tins. A short while later the Frisbee was born.

FABULOUS FRISBEE THROWS

The World Flying Disc Federation keeps track of official records for just about everything you can possibly do with a Frisbee. Here are the record holders for longest throw in several categories:

Man	Christian Voigt (Germany)	4/01/01	217.05 meters
Woman	Jennifer Griffin (USA)	4/08/00	138.56 meters
Child under six years old	Makoto Oshima (Japan)	9/05/93	43.23 meters
Human, caught by dog	Mark Molnar to Cheyenne-Ashley		
	(man to whippet, USA)	10/12/94	118.90 meters
Nonhuman	Alex (sea lion, USA)	12/05/96	9.76 meters

FRISBEE PHYSICS

The aerodynamics of a Frisbee in flight are quite complicated. Doctoral dissertations have been written on the interplay of lift, thrust, rotation, and gravity. But for our purposes, two concepts explain most of what we need to know.

The first is that a Frisbee is a *gyroscope*. There is a more complete explanation of gyroscopes in *Chapter 5: Ride a Bike*. Suffice it to say that a Frisbee—like a bicycle wheel or a skipping stone—tends to stay in one plane because it is spinning. That's why a lack of spin results in a wobbly, unstable throw.

The other concept is one we haven't dealt with before—the airfoil.

Air consists of billions of molecules of gas flying around and bumping into things. Even though we can't see them, all that bumping creates pressure—enough pressure to inflate a balloon or pop the top off a soda bottle.

Now, imagine an object that is flat on one side but curved on the other. This is called an airfoil. If we move it through the air, the molecules that go around the curved side have to travel farther than those that go around the flat side. That means they have to go faster.

In the mid-1700s a Swiss mathematician, Daniel Bernouli, described how this faster moving air exerts less pressure than air that is still. According to the "Bernouli principle," the air that moves over the curved top of a Frisbee doesn't push down as hard as the air underneath it pushes up. That's why, when a Frisbee flies, it hovers instead of dropping to the ground.

You can demonstrate this very quickly by turning a Frisbee upside down and throwing it. Notice how much quicker it drops? That's the Bernouli principle at work. But that's not all it does. The Bernouli principle is what makes eagles soar, airplanes fly, and sailboats sail, because wings and sails are actually airfoils. When it comes to aerodynamics, Bernouli rules!

A BERNOULI BRAINTEASER

Take a long strip of paper and hold one end just below your lips so the strip droops forward and down in front of your chin. What will happen to the paper when you blow air over the top of it? Think you know? Now try it.

GAMES

Go to a public park or a college campus almost anywhere in America and you'll see people doing amazing things with flying disks. Here are just a few examples:

Ultimate Frisbee

Think soccer with a Frisbee on a touch football field. Ultimate is a fast-paced, athletic, acrobatic, amazing sport. It requires a lot of running and good accuracy with a couple of basic throws, but most people catch on pretty quick.

Freestyle

If the Harlem Globetrotters used Frisbees instead of basketballs, they'd do freestyle. Usually, it involves rapidly spinning, floating tosses and complicated, acrobatic catches. Sometimes the bottom of the disk is sprayed with WD-40 to make it spin with less friction on the back of the player's outstretched fingernails. At its best, it's like Frisbee ballet.

Frisbee Golf

First, everyone grab a Frisbee. Go outside and find a target that's about three or four throws away. Take turns throwing your Frisbees, taking each subsequent throw from where the last one landed. Whoever hits the target in the fewest throws wins the hole. When all players are done, take a long sip of whatever beverage you happen to be holding and pick out another hole.

That, in its simplest form, is Frisbee golf. Of course, you can make it as easy or challenging, and as formal or casual, as you like. You can construct a course for any skill level, adding distance, obstacles, and doglegs as your and your child's skills improve.

Frisbee Fetch

Do you have a dog that loves to run, leap, and fetch? Congratulations! You will never lack for someone to play Frisbee with. Every year there are Frisbee dog competitions all over the country where the best, brightest, and furriest gather together to heave flying disks and snatch them out of the sky. If you can find one in your area, you should definitely go and take your kids. It's a hoot.

HOW SUZY SAVED THE WORLD

Two aliens named Warkon and Meekon were cruising around the galaxy in their flying saucer, looking for a planet to destroy. One day they came to the planet Earth.

"Look," said Warkon. "Our sensors show that this planet contains only primitive beings. Their technology is far inferior to ours. Let's conquer them and turn them into slaves."

"Wait," said Meekon, "we need more information. We should observe one of these beings for ourselves."

A moment later they were watching a young girl on their viewing screen. She was standing in a grassy park, laughing in the sunshine.

"Hah!" said Warkon. "It is weak and defenseless. Let's capture it and force it to give us information."

"Wait," said Meekon. "Look at *that*. What is it holding?"

They zoomed in for a closer view and saw that the girl held a flying saucer clenched in her hands.

"It has captured one of our ships!" said Meekon. "It must be gigantic!"

"No matter," said Warkon. "We have superior technology and intelligence. Our ship will escape easily."

Sure enough, the saucer flew out of the girl's hands and soared through the air. But just as the aliens were breathing a sigh of relief, a big German shepherd leaped up and snatched the saucer in its jaws. The dog rolled around in the grass, gnawing the saucer with its sharp teeth.

"Let's get out of here!" said Meekon.

"You can say that again!" said Warkon.

And they never bothered Earth again.

21
NAME THE STARS

> " 'Tis the witching hour of night,
> Orbed is the moon and bright,
> And the stars they glisten, glisten,
> Seeming with bright eyes to listen
> For what listen they?"
> —John Keats

Once, on the dubious advice of others, my father bought a little piece of property as a tax shelter. It was densely wooded and out in the middle of nowhere. One gray, November afternoon my family drove out to see it and to have a look around.

It was autumn and the woods were lovely, but no different from any others. After a while, when we'd had our fill of wandering through the trees, we headed back to our car. But after walking a little distance, we realized that we'd gone the wrong direction. We tried to retrace our steps, but no matter which way we turned, everything looked the same.

Eventually we found an abandoned dirt road that we hoped would lead us back to civilization. We followed it, as it forked and turned, for more than an hour before it dwindled to a footpath, then disappeared.

The light was fading fast, and my brothers and I were frightened. My parents tried to reassure us, but we could hear the worry in their voices and see it in their eyes. Finally, it got so dark we couldn't see where we were going. A cold, steady rain started to fall. We sat down under a big maple tree and huddled together for warmth.

A few hours before dawn, I woke up wet and shivering, with my head in my mother's lap. I lay there for a minute, trying to remember where I was.

The clouds had parted, and a few stars shone through the bare branches overhead. Three of the brightest were lined up in a row, and I recognized them as the belt of Orion. He was the one familiar thing in that strange and frightening place, and I was glad to see him. Under his watchful gaze, I drifted back to sleep.

Later that morning we emerged from the woods looking like a family of Asian refugees and startled a poor woman in her backyard. It was a fitting ending to the strangest night of my childhood.

These days, when I have trouble sleeping or I'm feeling a little lost, I sometimes go out for a late night walk by myself. If it's winter, I keep an eye on the southern sky and search for my old friend Orion. Even if the clouds don't part, I know he's up there watching.

WHEN TO START

To really enjoy stargazing, your kid has to be reasonably awake and alert at a late hour, patient enough to let his eyes adjust to the dark, and able to associate complex shapes and patterns on a star chart with those in the sky. Many kids can spot easy constellations by age five or six, but for a full-fledged outing, you might wait until they're a couple years older.

WHAT YOU NEED BEFORE YOU START

A Dark Sky

Light pollution is a stargazer's worst enemy. The more light you eliminate, the more stars you'll see. Start by choosing a night when the moon is new or a time when it hasn't risen yet. Turn off the porch lights and get away from street lamps and the bright lights of the city. Try viewing the sky over a large body of water. Even better, get out to where there are no city lights at all.

A Clear Sky

Obviously, this means no clouds, but it also means no mist or pollution. The clearest air is at high altitudes, where the atmosphere is thin and the humidity is low. In many places, the best stargazing happens in the winter when the air is dry, but then you have to contend with the cold.

You may want to make stargazing part of a vacation in the mountains, where the air and the darkness bring the stars out by the millions.

Time

It takes fifteen to twenty minutes for your eyes to fully adjust to the darkness. Take your time. Remember, you're up in the middle of the night with your kid in your lap, staring at the sky. Enjoy.

Warm Clothes

Unless you plan to keep your kids up way past bedtime, you'll end up doing a lot of stargazing during the winter. The early darkness and the crisp, clear air are perfect, as long as you're prepared for the cold.

You may be out there for a while, and you won't be moving around much. Bring more clothes than you think you need, and bring a blanket too. A thermos full of hot chocolate isn't a bad idea either.

Folding Chairs

There's nothing that'll send you home faster than a wet butt on a cold night. Enough said.

Star Chart

If you want to go beyond the simple constellations named in this chapter, a star chart is invaluable. There are plenty out there—in books, at toy stores, and even on the Internet. I like the plastic ones that spin around and adjust according to the date and the time. Get one that's big enough to read in dim light.

One great trick is to bring a flashlight covered with some red cellophane, held on by a rubber band. The red light allows you to see the star chart without messing up your night vision.

Binoculars or Telescope

These are fun, but strictly optional. They help with faint stars and they give a great view of near objects like the moon, but they can be frustrating for young kids, who never seem to get them focused and pointed straight at the same time.

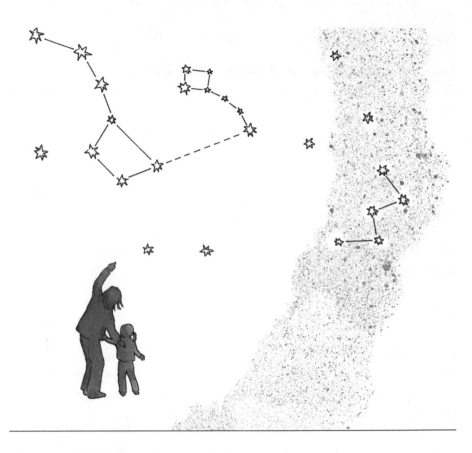

BASIC TECHNIQUE

Basic Principles

When we look up at the sky from the Northern Hemisphere of our planet, it's as if we were sitting in a big room on a gigantic, spinning ball. The North Pole points directly at the North Star, which is also called Polaris. As the Earth rotates, the other stars seem to spin around Polaris. These constellations to the north are always in our view, because we are sitting on top of the spinning ball, and they're up on the ceiling.

Now imagine that we're looking downward at a spot on the floor. Since we're on top of the ball, we can't look straight down, because the ball is in the way. Instead, we look down and off to the side. As the ball spins, the floor seems to spin around us, and the spot comes in and out of view.

This is what happens when we look at the southern sky. These constellations come into view for only part of each day. But for half the year, they're on the same side of Earth as the sun and they move through our sky during daylight. Only during the other half of the year can we see them at night. That's why every southern constellation has a peak viewing season. Orion, for example, is best seen in wintertime.

Your star chart will help you figure out which stars are in the southern sky on certain nights and what time to look for them. But for a start, let's look at the constellations to the north that are always in view.

The Big Dipper

This is one of the easiest constellations to find. Its seven main stars are among the brightest in the northern sky, and they form the unmistakable shape of a ladle or pot. Refer to the diagram to see the shape, but re member that it may be rotated, depending on the time of night and time of year, and it could be just above the horizon or much higher in the sky.

This group of stars is part of the constellation known as Ursa Major—the Great Bear. As with most constellations, it's hard to see the shape of what it's supposed to represent. When Ursa Major is drawn, the handle of the dipper is usually portrayed as a tail, which makes it look more like a lemur than a bear. Go figure.

According to Roman myth, the Great Bear was once the maiden Callisto. Like so many mortals before her, she was caught up in a web of deceit and jealousy by the impetuous, all-powerful gods. In the end, the goddess Juno transformed her into a bear, and she was almost killed by her own unsuspecting son, Arcas. At the last second, Jupiter intervened. He changed Arcas into a bear as well, and transported them both to the heavens as the constellations Ursa Major and Ursa Minor.

The Little Dipper and Polaris

In the bowl of the Big Dipper, the two stars farthest from the handle are known as the "Pointer Stars." This is because they point directly at Polaris. In your mind's eye, draw a line from the Pointer Star at the bottom of the bowl to the one at the rim, and keep going. The next medium-bright star you reach will be the North Star. As long as humans have sailed the seas, sailors have used this star to navigate by dark of night.

Polaris is the last star in the handle of the Little Dipper, which is also known as Ursa Minor. The Little Dipper has a similar shape to the Big Dipper, only upside down and with its handle pointed in the opposite direction. It looks as if one might be pouring water into the other.

As I mentioned above, Ursa Minor was once Arcas, the son of Callisto. As it turns out, he and his mother were not free from Juno's jealous wrath even after Jupiter turned them into constellations. Juno, with the help of the sea god Neptune, forbade Ursa Major and Ursa Minor from ever bathing in the ocean. This is why they circle the northern sky every night, never dipping below the horizon. Apparently, neither one has had a bath for thousands of years. Yuck. We're talking serious bear B.O.

Cassiopeia

If you follow the line from the Pointer Stars to Polaris, then veer right about 30 degrees and keep going, you'll see five stars clustered together to form a W or M. This is Cassiopeia.

According to legend, Cassiopeia was a legendary beauty and queen of Ethiopia. In a moment of monumental stupidity, she boasted that she was more beautiful than Juno herself. Bad idea. Again, Juno went to her go-to guy Neptune, who sent a terrible sea monster to swallow Ethiopia whole. In the end, a guy named Perseus killed the monster, and everything turned out okay. Still, you have to wonder what Cassiopeia was thinking. Whatever you do, don't mess with Juno on a bad-hair day.

The Milky Way

If you're out on a dark, clear night, far from city lights, you'll notice that Cassiopeia sits right in the middle of a faint arc of light that sweeps across the sky. This is the Milky Way. It runs roughly perpendicular to the line from Polaris to Cassiopeia.

The Milky Way isn't *one* thing—it's billions of things. It's actually our galaxy. Try this. Take a broad, flat container made of clear glass, like a pie plate. Fill it with an inch of water and add a few drops of milk—just enough to make it slightly cloudy. If you look down through the top of the water, you can see through it pretty well. But when you look at it through the side, it looks much more solid and white.

Our galaxy is shaped like that flat disk of water and milk, and we're in the middle of it. When we look toward the edge of the disk, we see a greater concentration of stars, and it looks like a streak across the sky. That's the Milky Way.

Reading Star Charts

Now that we know a few constellations around the North Star, we can use them to explore the rest of the sky. It's time to get out your star chart. Don't forget to put the red cellophane on your flashlight so it doesn't mess up your night vision.

Star charts are round, and they represent the entire dome of stars above the horizon. For this reason, things that appear close together on the chart will seem farther apart in the sky. For instance, when the Big Dipper is low over the northern horizon, Cassiopeia is nearly directly overhead. A chart is specific for a certain date and a certain time of night. If you have an adjustable chart, make sure you set it correctly.

Step 1

Start by finding the North Star. Face toward it and hold your chart so the edge labeled "North" is at the bottom. The center of the circle shows the stars directly above you. The top edge of the circle is the southern horizon behind you.

Step 2

Now that you're oriented, start with a constellation you know, like the Big Dipper. Work your way upward, or around the horizon, identifying new constellations as you go. At first it's hard to pick out the stars in a constellation from the many dimmer stars that aren't part of the pattern. Most star charts indicate the relative brightness of stars. Pay attention to this—it helps a lot. If you can identify one or two of the brightest stars, the rest of the constellation usually falls into place.

If you're looking for a star that isn't very bright, try looking off to the side a little. We pick up dim light better with our peripheral vision. (See *Chapter 8: Juggle* for more on peripheral vision.)

Step 3

Try to find some of the constellations from the zodiac. See if you can find your sign in the sky. And don't forget the Milky Way—it's a great landmark when you can't figure out where you are.

"SO, WHAT'S YOUR SIGN?"

Some of the brightest objects in the sky aren't stars at all—they're planets. Before people realized this, planets were looked upon as "wandering stars." While the stars remain fixed in their constellations, planets arc across the sky in patterns that have intrigued philosophers and scientists for centuries.

Because all the planets orbit in more or less the same plane, they always move across our sky through the same arc of constellations. These, of course, are represented in the signs of the zodiac. By watching the comings and goings of the planets through these twelve constellations, astrologers throughout the ages have tried to divine the influence of the planets on our lives.

Of course, we now know that the stars are no more fixed in place than the planets are. They only seem to stand still because they're so far away. As a matter of fact, they're just as far from each other as they are from us. The grouping of the stars into constellations is an illusion. The stars in a particular group may be millions of light-years from each other, but they appear to be together because we view them from only a certain angle.

WHY DO STARS TWINKLE?

When we look at the stars, we view them through miles and miles of the Earth's atmosphere. All that air, with its different layers of density swirling and flowing above us, distorts the light that passes through it and causes it to flicker. It's like lying on your back on the bottom of a swimming pool and looking up at someone who's leaning over the water.

If we went up in a spaceship and left the Earth's atmosphere, the stars wouldn't seem to twinkle anymore. That's why scientists sent the

Hubble space telescope into orbit. Without all that distortion, it lets them see things they could never see from Earth.

WHAT ARE FALLING STARS?

Though most of our solar system has no atmosphere, it isn't empty. It's filled with floating particles that range in size from specks of dust to big chunks of rock. These particles are called meteors.

When a meteor hits our outer atmosphere, it does so at about 140,000 mph. As it plunges through all the molecules of gas, it rubs against them and causes friction, which creates heat. It's like when you rub your hands together to keep them warm, only much more intense. Meteors create so much heat that they burn up, and then we see them as "falling stars." The bigger the particle, the more spectacular the show, but most meteors are no bigger than a grain of sand.

Some parts of the solar system have more dust and particles than others. These are often trails that were left behind by ancient comets. A comet is just a big ball of ice and particles that circles the sun. When it passes near the sun, it melts and leaves behind a trail of dust that we see as its tail. Long after the comet leaves, the particles remain.

When the Earth's orbit passes through an old comet trail, we're treated to a "meteor shower." The best known is the Perseid shower, which occurs over several days and peaks on August 12, yielding about fifty meteors an hour. It's named after Perseus, who saved Cassiopeia's kingdom from the sea monster. That's because the meteors in this shower seem to radiate from his constellation, which is on the Milky Way right next to Cassiopeia.

There are other major showers that peak on January 3, October 21, and December 14. These are great times to take your kids stargazing. You can search for constellations while you count falling stars.

HOW MANY STARS ARE IN THE SKY?

That's a question every child asks at least once. Now you can answer it!

No one knows how many stars there are in the universe, because some may be too dim or far away for us to see. But astronomers have calculated how many stars are within the reach of our most powerful telescopes. They did it by counting the number of galaxies in a known portion of the sky and estimating the number of stars in each galaxy. Here's the final estimate: 70,000,000,000,000,000,000,000. That's seventy sextillion—almost ten thousand times as many stars as there are grains of sand on all the beaches in the world!

HOW ABOUT "FURRIUS, THE HAMSTER"?

The Greeks aren't the only ones who saw pictures in the night. Many cultures have had their own constellations, often with completely different stars than the ones we group together today. As a matter of fact, no one owns exclusive naming rights to the heavens. Everything up there is in the public domain. So when your kids have found all the constellations they can, have them make up a few of their own. They can even make up myths to go along with them.

Here's an idea—the next time a family pet dies, why not give it its own constellation? You and your kids can go out and look for its likeness in the sky. Mark down the location on your star chart so you can find it again whenever you want. Even if Sparky the goldfish had a Ty-D-Bol burial at sea, his memory can live on among the stars.

STUPID STARGAZING JOKES

Q: What snacks should you take when you go stargazing?
A: Mars bars and Milky Ways.

Q: How many astronomers does it take to change a lightbulb?
A: None, astronomers prefer the dark.

Q: Why do aliens make good stargazers?
A: They have 20–20–20 vision.

*   *   *

"When I grow up," said Billy, "I want to travel to the sun."

"That's impossible," said Kate. "The sun's rays would burn you to a crisp!"

"That's okay," said Billy. "I'll travel at night."

*   *   *

A group of tourists became lost in the jungle, and they were captured by a tribe of cannibals.

"Don't worry," said one of them. "I am an astronomer, and I happen to know that there will be a lunar eclipse at precisely 10:56 tonight. I will pretend to be a god and threaten to make the moon disappear. When it does, they will cower in fear and set us free."

"But what if they eat us before then?" asked one of the others.

Their guide, who knew the cannibals' language, called out to one of the guards and spoke with him.

"What did he say?" asked the astronomer.

"He says that usually they would eat us at sunset, but tonight is the night of the great feast, so they won't eat us until midnight."

"That's perfect!" said the astronomer. "What a stroke of luck! Why are they having this feast?"

"To celebrate the lunar eclipse."

About the Author

JEFFREY LEE lives, works, and plays with his wife and two daughters in Seattle, Washington. He writes fiction and nonfiction for both children and adults. His novel *True Blue* (for ages ten and up) was published by Delacorte Press in the fall of 2003.

Dr. Lee is a graduate of Stanford University and Harvard Medical School. He trained in family medicine at the University of Washington, with a special emphasis on family dynamics.

For the past sixteen years, Dr. Lee has cared for thousands of families at an inner-city community clinic. He has led workshops in writing and drama in the Seattle public schools, and has coached baseball, soccer, and tennis with children of all ages. At various times in his speckled past he has worked as a playground monitor, a cook, a gardener, and a carpenter. But mostly he'd rather be fishing.